For Love, Money, and Future Considerations

by Mel Profit

Photographs by Terry Hancey

Designed by Ken Rodmell

D.C. Heath Canada Ltd.,
Toronto

For The Friends of Mousey Brown.

Contents

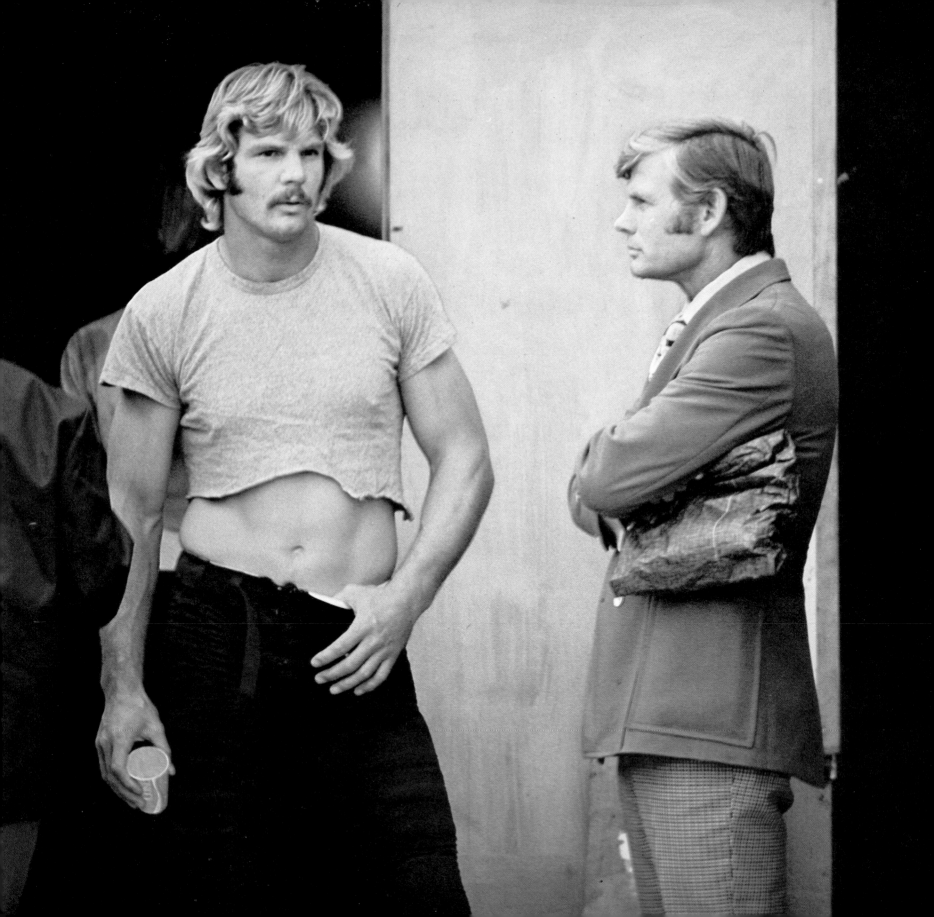

Foreword

Reading Mel Profit's book, For Love, Money, and Future Considerations, took me back to my own playing days, and I relived entire seasons. Everything is there: the training camp where it all begins, and sometimes ends; the injuries you have to live with, maybe for the rest of your life; the time spent before a game just waiting; the games themselves and the self-evaluation after; and that big football dream, the Grey Cup.

Mel looks back over his career, which has been an outstanding one, and makes it real for his readers. As the old cliche goes, "He tells it like it is". Terry Hancey's photographs, the best of the six thousand he took during the 1971 season, do the same. Words are inadequate to really express what playing football means to the pro. How do you explain personal feelings or the instincts that cause a player to make his moves at the right or wrong time? The exceptional photographs in this book, however, enable the reader to sense from the expressions and movements caught there what a frustrating as well as rewarding sport football is.

This is not intended to be an instructional book for youngsters, but it could be one for adults who, after all, determine to a large extent how young would-be players see the game. For this book clearly shows the glory, and the price a pro has to pay to attain it.

I hope Mel will excuse the very personal tone of what I've written and will accept my congratulations on a book that is outstanding in both content and design. I hope all his readers will find in it the enjoyment and the food for thought that I did.

Dick Shatto

Introduction

In a sense, this book is nearly five years old. That's how long it's been since I first thought of putting it together.

It took the first three years just to meet the other two people who had the ability and enthusiasm necessary to turn out the finished product.

I met Ken Rodmell before he left his position as Art Director of The Canadian Magazine to try the world on his own. I am, as I think many readers are, familiar with the design concepts employed in The Canadian, and that was recommendation enough. When I first heard about Ken, he was described as having a moustache and a beautiful wife, and he played touch football on the weekends. I figured, oh well, two out of three's not bad.

Finding out about Terry Hancey was easy. In talking to various newspaper people, particularly photographers, Terry kept being recommended as the best sports photographer available. Just plain finding Terry was another problem. There were to be times during the season when Ken and I would beat our heads in frustration because there was some important aspect of the game we wanted Terry to concentrate on, and we couldn't even reach him by telephone. Then he'd get whatever it was we wanted anyway and evaporate again. As it turned out, the final pictorial selection for this book was culled from over 6,000 shots.

This is not a conventional sports book. Our objective was to present a pictorial tribute to our brand of football, one that showed as honestly as possible the people, the beauty, and the pain that make up the game.

The supporting text is a personal reflection on my life as a Canadian Football League player. Our prime concern was to maintain a proper balance between positive and negative because that, I think, is where the game of professional football is located. So while it too is a tribute to strengths of the sport, it is also an acknowledgment of weaknesses.

A word about the title. When a team wants to get rid of a player of any value, they trade him for equal value. Sometimes, if they have to or want to get rid of him bad enough, they give him to the team least likely to haunt them for their generosity. The trade is then made for a favour which is given the nebulous title "future considerations". I don't think it's any secret that for the past couple of years I've lived with the rumour of an impending trade. It's been a somewhat shaky but interesting challenge in my life to see if I could beat it or if, in the end, someone just might get me for future considerations.

Peace,
Mel Profit
April, 1972

Part 1

The Necessary Evil

Chapter 1

The first sage I met in pro football was the player who told me, "Never unpack your suitcase". He was the starting offensive centre, a five year veteran. He was traded less than a week later.

I was only about twelve or thirteen when I first started to play football and when an equally young girl said one of those beautiful things you remember all your life. It was, "If God wanted you to play football, you'd have been born with a helmet". I wrote her off as a religious fanatic. But the older I get the more I wonder if she knew something I didn't know. I think about that every year when I report to training camp.

There's very little that remains constant for a football player. Every training camp starts a new lifetime. It can mean a new team, or a new coach, or at the very least new faces, often a number greater than that of those you recognize. It can also mean your first chance or your last chance, because in a field where the average career lasts only about four years, there isn't much in between.

From any viewpoint, training camp is the single most demanding period of the season. And it's not just physically demanding; that's obvious. The demand it makes and the value it has depends a great deal on a person's situation, that is, on whether he's a coach, rookie, or veteran.

For the coaching staff, training camp is the only time they have to evaluate personnel and instill the technical proficiency necessary to perform as a team. You'll also hear some occasional rubbish about how necessary it is for conditioning. A player can just as easily get in shape on his own.

The rookie faces the most difficult job. It's his only opportunity to impress the boss with his ability and/or importance as a player. There are more contingencies that can affect the outcome than he could ever have imagined when he made the choice to turn pro. The first lesson he learns is the reality of the business of professional football. Most players coming out of college are conditioned to the idea that participation is its own reward and many find it hard to handle the professional philosophy "We know what you did for us yesterday, but what have you done for us recently?". Normally a rookie has to compete against a veteran who has had a season or more to prove himself. And he faces the problem of personalities. It's not the easiest time to make friends considering it's a "me or the other guy" situation.

Maintaining your confidence is the biggest battle. As soon as you begin to doubt yourself it's time to pack. It's not simply a matter of doubting your own ability, since generally there is little difference in the relative ability of the men who qualify for professional football at any given position. It's more a matter of emotional outlook.

In 1964, I reported to my first pro training camp as physically and mentally prepared as I thought possible. In the first few days I played well and was made to feel comfortable by the coaching staff, but prior to the exhibition games I pulled a muscle and had to sit out nearly two weeks. That was the beginning of a long fall. I was rarely acknowledged in that time and I thought they had taken a pass on me. The pulled muscle eventually healed enough for me to start working out again but at never much more than half speed. I was pressing hard to make up for it, but my mind just came apart. By the end of camp I was so psyched out I couldn't even play catch on the sidelines without dropping the ball.

Surprisingly, that's not an isolated case. Marv Luster was an All-America end in college and then an all-star receiver in his first years with the Montreal Alouettes. Marv had the same problem and Montreal simply released him. He came to Toronto in 1964 for nothing more than the standard $350 league waiver fee.

The pressure has been eased somewhat for rookies over the past few years. There have been many cases recently where the only players guaranteed jobs were in fact people who had never set foot on a field as pros. In the locker room idiom, pros refer to a player who misses a contest as having had a perfect game,. i.e. no mistakes. Rookies being guaranteed jobs seems to fit right in with that way of thinking.

From a vet's standpoint training camp is pretty much a case of "everything to lose" since it's a question of fighting to retain what has already been earned. In many ways the situation is analogous to the fabled gunfight, with the old veteran facing the kid, the new gun in town. There's always someone who wants to be the fastest gun. And the truth is, eventually there's someone faster than you.

After the first year I had no desire to try training camp or football again, so in 1965 I gave it up. It didn't prove to be so easy; after a summer of travelling in Europe, I found I actually missed playing.

That December in Vancouver, I signed a contract with the B.C. Lions, then returned to Los Angeles to have my third knee operation, something I'd neglected to mention to B.C.

After the operation I spent the winter supported by disability insurance, living on hot dogs and beans and protein supplements that university friends stole from the athletic department. In the morning I lifted weights to strengthen my leg and every afternoon ran miles along isolated stretches of beach.

By June my knee was stronger than it had ever been. I was in the best condition of my life, and my weight, something I can lose as quickly as most people put it on, was up to 240 pounds. Everything was right.

At least everything was right until I reported to the Lions. As soon as I arrived I started receiving suggestions to cut my hair. These came not only from the management, but from some players as well. As it turned out, I became Toronto property before the season got under way and the management here was too busy trying to field a team to bother about the length of my hair. At least the first year. On road trips, however, particularly out West, I had problems. Coming onto the field in Regina I had to keep my helmet on because there were a few demonstrative fans standing on both sides of the players' entrance trying to tell me how they felt by bouncing various objects off my head.

It was one of those earlier training camps when I first got turned on to football mythology, the bits that have been built around some inconsequential factor to heighten the entertainment value or mystique of the game. The line that hooked me, and is my favourite myth as a pass receiver, was "This guy throws a hard pass". Of course there's also "This guy throws a soft pass", or "This guy lets the ball hang" and others you can still hear on T.V. from most any analyst or commentator. Standing around playing catch you can notice the difference in velocity with which one quarterback throws the ball compared to another, but in a game you couldn't tell the difference if the pass had a sign on it. When a receiver says a quarterback "throws a hard pass to catch", don't worry about the quarterback, but don't make any bets on that receiver.

One of the irritating facts I have to accept in training camp is the workload of a tight end. The emphasis given to any particular drill depends on whether you are a lineman or a back. Hitting drills are usually tougher for linemen because hitting is their primary function. Running drills are usually tougher for the backs for the same reason. A tight end is something of a mutation, part lineman, part back, so he usually gets grouped with the linemen during hitting drills and with backs when it comes time to run. When I was about thirteen years old, in my first year of football, I got a hint of how much I was going to like such an arrangement. My coach said, "Profit, you can't catch, you can't block and you can't tackle. Just what is your specialty?"

Tight end is something of a unique position because of the variety of demands made on the job in a highly specialized game. A number of pro scouts have gone on record as stating the most difficult positions to fill in pro ball are quarterback, middle linebacker, and tight end.

Training camps must be the most monotonous places in the world. One of the most erudite definitions of camp went something like, "If signing a pro contract is the marriage of man to football, then training camp is that perfectly isolated honeymoon spot where there is nothing else to do but consummate the deal". There's a standard joke based on the idea that, in searching for training camp sites, managements make a list of all locations in order of their desirability, then pick the one on the bottom. There's also a curious but acceptable assumption that monastic retreats receive some sort of priority. Most players can remember part of a summer spent knocking heads at a St. Joe's or a St. Mike's. I think coaches at those locations have historically felt that should things get a little out of hand, they need only call down His wrath. When I got here in 1966 I was told Bob Shaw had it written in his contract. Leo Cahill also talked to Him, just before the 1969 play-offs but apparently there was a communications breakdown. We were destroyed by "an act of God" known as the Ottawa Rough Riders.

Repetition brings on boredom, and both are established fact in training camp. You can pick up a quick education from the people who've been through it before, and one of the early lessons is that in order to stay sane, you've got to be a little crazy. Madness takes on all shapes and sizes, but one of its expressions common to all camps is the midnight run.

I think "midnight run" is pretty well self-explanatory. In essence it is what happens after the nightly curfew, usually around 10:00 or 11:00 p.m.

The leading exponent of the midnight run in my days was Bobby Taylor. Bobby just plain wasn't ready for 11:00 p.m. bedchecks. We wouldn't necessarily hear him leave, but we usually knew when he got back. He had a casual way of announcing his return, like turning on the fire alarm at 2:00 or 3:00 a.m.

A by-product of training camp regimentation is the kind of humour that results. There are no outside distractions or diversions so you have to create your own. The end result doesn't always sound like what you might expect from adults.

In Vancouver, a player received instant notoriety when he accepted the terms of a bet made by some teammates at a restaurant during a break from work-outs. Ignoring his sandwich he took a bite from the north end of the waitress as she was headed south. Incidentally, she sued. And won.

One of Toronto's favourite stories involves a rookie quarterback who brought his new girl back to camp from the local pub in which they had just met. It was after curfew so they decided to remain in the parking lot and adjourned to the first convenient car where they were soon surprised by the owner, who happened to be the head coach. The quarterback was eventually cut.

The locker room becomes the focal point of the camp. More information, fact or fiction, is disseminated from this one spot than from any other. From the time an individual enters camp to the time he leaves it, nothing from the outside world is sacred . . . . be it God, mother, country or coach.

"Tradewinds" are an example of locker room humour. Every year during camp rumours of possible or pending trades fill the media. More often than not they prove false, but they help sell newspapers and make for good coffee-break conversations, so they persist. In the locker room, tradewinds are always blowing. And the more insulting the trade may be to your teammate involved, the more popular the trade. It's also the place where roles are reversed and players trade management. Usually the trades result in material gain . . . the General Manager for a pair of roller skates . . . . . in as much as players regard management in general as being pretty much on the same stereotyped level as a used car salesman.

In 1971, the media headlined an impending trade that saw Dave Raimey and me headed for the B.C. Lions. We found out about it at 7:30 in the morning when we picked up a newspaper at breakfast during the first week of training camp. And both of us were annoyed to say the least. David had been the second best rusher in the conference the previous season, but was considered expendable because he'd had an "off" year. Any other back in the conference would have been ecstatic to have an "on" year as good as David's "off" year. I was considered expendable because some levels of management considered me a bad guy.

We talked over the situation and decided if we had to go we were going to go smiling, mainly because that tends to drive your enemies crazy. So

15

for the workout that morning, we showed up on the practice field wearing B.C. decals taped to our helmets, extolling the virtues of the West Coast. The "trade" promptly died.

One of the greatest running gags I ever heard was introduced in 1967 by a lineman named Kent Francisco. He patterned a monologue titled Argo Place after the T.V. soap opera version of Peyton Place, incorporating the team and coaching staff in his cast of characters. And in the face of a five win, nine loss record, any relief we could get with "Will the lovely Leo Cahill reunite with Little Bobby Taylor, or will the latest attack of hearthburn force the Modest Mentor to seek solace......." was savoured every day in the Never Ending Saga of Argo Place. Francisco however, felt he saw the handwriting on the wall and retired at the end of the season.

Argo Place retained its popularity because its content was based on fact. Every club qualifies for its own satire. The status of each individual in a football community is constantly being evaluated by the other members. The pecking order changes on both the management and player levels in the same way it does in politics or on a restaurant staff. And if it weren't for the rumours and gossip surrounding these changes, football would be a drag off the field.

The "numbers game", the rule that dictates roster content by nationality, creates a situation unique to the C.F.L., one that affects both players and coaches. Prior to 1972 a maximum of 14 Americans could be carried by any one team and the remaining 18 had to be Canadian. Early in 1972 the League took a step backward by changing to a 15-17 ratio. By decreasing the Canadian number, particularly at a time when more and more outstanding Canadians are entering the league, this new rule creates the impression that C.F.L. management thinks of Canadians as second class athletes.

The value obtained by changing the nationality of one player is really negligible. The only significant roster change would have been to increase the 32 man limit. With the present small rosters, it only takes a few injuries to significantly reduce the entertainment value of our game. In the C.F.L. 24 players start in any game. In the N.F.L. only 22 start, yet each team carries a 40 man roster as well as a reserve or "taxi" squad. If the C.F.L. were to add one Canadian player per year, by 1980 it would have not only a comparable 40 man squad but provide employment for 72 additional Canadian players without changing the import quota. And assuming an expansion of facilities as well as improved television revenue over that period, the addition of one player per year certainly seems economically feasible.

Each year sometime prior to May 31, all ballplayers except those already signed for the coming season receive a registered letter from their club that reads something like, "Pursuant to Article 15 of your Contract ... we hereby give you notice that we are renewing said Contract for a further term ... at 90% of the rate of compensation in said Contract as provided and on the terms set forth". Which all means that the Club is exercising the option clause (Article 15) in your contract and you can either take a 10% pay cut and play for another year, or quit.

The option letter is normally just a formality that precedes negotiations on a new contract, but it's irritating as hell to be reminded with such coldness that chattels still exist.

One of my fondest dreams was that before I left football somebody with a little imagination would infiltrate the management level and I would one day open that registered letter and read "Gotcha!"

Contracts and salaries have improved tremendously in the past few years, but these improvements have pretty well centred around incoming players. One thing younger players brought with them that benefitted all players was the concept of personal managers. In the beginning management resistance to dealing with a player's representative instead of the player was pretty strong. There are many cases where clubs have refused to acknowledge such representation. I don't think there ever was a logical reason. The reaction was based on tradition more than anything else. I am not sure that personal managers have much value, except in the odd case, but I could never understand why football franchises, which have business and legal representation on their payroll, would deny the same help to a player who was often involved in the first major business transaction in his life.

Actually, one of the best reasons for having someone else do the negotiating is that you can then avoid personal confrontations with people you work for that may carry over onto the field. It's tough enough surviving training camp without being mad at the world for the "indignities" that can occur when it comes time to hassle about money.

At the end of our first training camp workout in 1968, Leo Cahill asked me to drop by his office and get my contract out of the way. I didn't think there'd be any problem and told him what I wanted. Before turning around and walking off he said, "Last year you turned from sugar to shit and you're asking for that kind of money!" Two months later, the day after our first league game, I received exactly the contract I asked for. Since then I've always thought it was a pretty funny line.

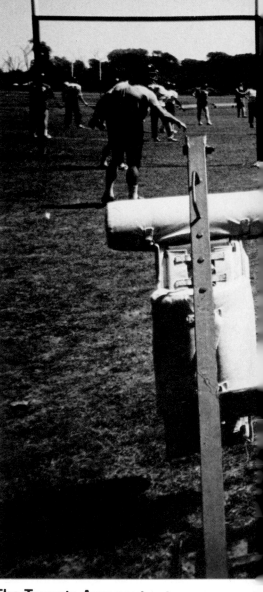

The Toronto Argonauts at their St. Andrews training camp in Aurora, fifty miles from Toronto. Twice a day we scar the beauty of the country.
Coach Leo Cahill watches the 9:00 a.m. workout from his personal tower.
The primary purpose of these camps is to isolate the people involved, the idea being the fewer the distractions the more time to think football. I guess it never occurred to any-

body that we would spend a great deal of time thinking about those things we've been isolated from. The whole period takes on an "it will all be over with soon" attitude. You try to shut your mind to it and just react because the process is based on repetition, and repetition becomes boredom. Before every practice, the same thought goes through my mind: In a couple of hours, it'll all be over.

It's kind of paradoxical, those first few minutes after a practice has ended. You practice to learn, but I don't think most players unlock their minds until it's over. Maybe it isn't thinking that's locked out so much as feeling. Afterwards, there's not only time for your son but for the defensive end who was trying to take your head off minutes earlier as well.

21

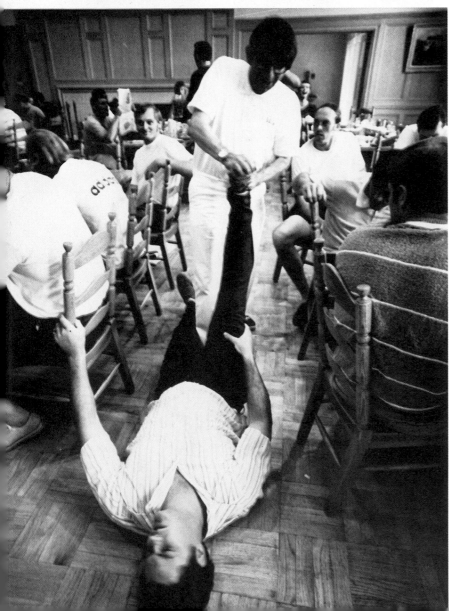

Tradition rules the system—
even training table where
the coaches sit segregated
from the players at a head
table.
One of the few traditions
carried on by players,
even though it is seen only
occasionally now, is that
of rookies singing during
the meal. Initially they
were required to sing
their school song, but now
anything goes. And it can
be either a humourous
or painful experience.
Some people take over the
place not because of any
singing ability but with
sheer determination. Occasionally, you'll hear an
ovation, as in the case of
John Trainor, Joe Theismann,
and Ed Williams; but more
often you'll hear booing.
Loud booing.
I've never been in a camp
where the food wasn't close
to excellent. But it's difficult to appreciate it and
sometimes difficult just
to eat when you feel wiped
out. The highlight of the
evening is watching the
trainer trying to help a
player suffering from
leg cramps.

At one time or another, just about every man who plays the game has to tell someone it's over, that he didn't make it.

Toronto Argonauts leave their training camp field in Aurora after the last two-a-day workout at St. Andrews College in 1971. Half a dozen players would be released before they convened again in Toronto.

The Generals

Chapter 2

I've been asked if, when I quit playing, I would be interested in coaching. I doubt if I'd consider it on a professional level. I can't conceive of a less secure, less rewarding job, although sometimes I think the same thing about being a player.

Maybe this will illustrate the point. Just six years after I entered the league not one C.F.L. head coach remained at the job he had when I arrived. B.C. had been through four coaches while at least two other clubs had seen three.

Granted, men like Hamilton's Ralph Sazio, B.C.'s Jackie Parker and Ottawa's Frank Clair had moved up to management positions, but the fact remains all nine teams had made at least one turnover in six years. That's not how I would define security.

How important is a coach? He's the most important member in the franchise right up to the kick-off. Then, if he's done his job, you should be able to lock him up in the john and play out the game as if he were there.

Essentially, a football team is the extension of a coach's personality. He designs the technical framework, based on his offensive and defensive philosophy, which the team will incorporate. He scouts and often recruits most of the personnel brought in to make up the team. And he has sole responsibility for determining which individuals will comprise the final squad and carry out his design.

What goes into making a successful coach? Obviously there isn't any formula, or all coaches would be the same. In fact they're quite different.

Ray Jauch of the Eskimos: Coach of the year in 1970.

The late Vince Lombardi turned the Green Bay Packers into the best team in football for nearly a decade. He is considered the prototype of the

27

Argonaut Coach Leo Cahill
and Chairman John Bassett
on the field at Empire
Stadium before the 1971
Grey Cup game.

29

"successful" coach. A lot of people take as gospel one of his most famous quotes, "Winning isn't everything, it's the only thing". That may be economically correct in professional football, but somebody with a great deal more insight said a long time ago, "It's not whether you win or lose, but how you play the game". It's a trite expression, but it goes a great deal further toward defining "successful" in my mind than does Lombardi's philosophy. Winning isn't everything, and when it becomes the only thing it's a sickness.

The fact that there is no formula for success is underscored by the differences in the personalities of those who have coached championship teams. In the early 1960's the Winnipeg Blue Bombers won Grey Cups under Bud Grant. Bud gave the impression of being emotionally removed from the proceedings, whether during a practice, a game, or an interview. Players who worked for him then still refer to him as "the iceman".

Bud is a hunter and many people were convinced his first love wasn't football but his hunting dogs. Dave Raimey, an all star running back and Dick Thornton, an all star defensive halfback while in Winnipeg, still tell this training table story: When the Blue Bombers would have steak for dinner, Bud Grant would rise at the end of his meal and make his way down the tables with a fork in one hand and a bag in the other collecting the scraps for his dogs. When they saw him coming, those who weren't finished would start chewing like crazy because they knew there wasn't any second chance.

Just before he moved up, Frank Clair took Ottawa to the Grey Cup in 1968 and 1969, winning both times. He earned the nickname "Professor" for which he had both the appearance and demeanour. He had an unusual habit of referring to players by their football numbers instead of name. It wasn't, "Garney Henley did this or that", but rather, "That number 26...". A football critique came out like a math equation.

The physical gap between the players' room and the coaches' room may be only a few feet wide, but it might as well be an ocean. Traditionally coaches purposely created that gap; the wider the gap the more obvious the command. The more recent but limited concept is to narrow that space and improve communications between players and coaches. The greatest weakness in pro ball has always been the lack of communication. As in the military, you don't communicate, you command.

The military orientation is also evident in the fact that the traditional and still generally expected method of address by a player to a member of the staff is "Coach". It's comparable in the outside world to calling someone

"General". I think there are coaches who harbour a secret grudge against the military for monopolizing the act of saluting. I know a lot of them would dig a snappy salute with every "Yes, Coach".

When Toronto faced Montreal in the 1970 exhibition season, a number of Alouette players mentioned that Sam Etcheverry asked them to call him either by his first name or "Coach", whichever was most comfortable to them. In many cases it was the first time they had been given the option since entering football.

The word I heard most often used to describe Sam Etcheverry in his first season was "poise". It was used in connection with his public as well as game appearances. In the end I think that poise won the Grey Cup for his team. The Alouettes kept together while everyone else came unstuck. Sam's feat was doubly remarkable in that not only was it his initial year of C.F.L. coaching, but he won with a young, inexperienced club, just the kind that tradition says lacks poise.

If you've ever watched Calgary's Jim Duncan, on the field or even on T.V., you can see the energy. I watched him in the off-season working the banquet circuit and it was still there, gregariousness with a kind of balanced aggression. He doesn't overwhelm people, but he's always coming at you.

His football is much the same. Consistently a great passing team, Calgary developed a running game to match in 1971. Only Winnipeg had as smooth an offence in the league that year. And Calgary's defence is always coming at you.

Leo Cahill came to coach Toronto in 1967, after the Argos had finished dead last for about 5 years. The league's doormat immediately started on its way back up, but we did nothing to tarnish the Toronto reputation of being the C.F.L.'s oddball franchise.

The team he inherited consisted of a few very good football players and some very bad. They were the remnants of an airlift carried on over the previous two years that reportedly saw over 200 different players in a Toronto uniform. Players who survived that period said it was like training in an airport terminal.

The press built us up as a bunch of rebels and rejects. There was obviously some truth in it and we made it work for us. That was our bond. Leo fit right in—no impressive credentials and a "Who's he?" greeting. He'd successfully coached the Toronto Rifles, a minor league team that folded after a couple of years, but this was his first big job.

31

In a few minutes, Jim Duncan's Calgary Stampeders will be 1971 Grey Cup champions. Right now they have only a three point lead.

33

We wanted to get ready in a hurry and start winning right away. And we did. We had a great camp and an impressive exhibition season. Unfortunately, we were about the only ones playing it for keeps then. Once league play got under way, we bombed. But we still made it to the play-offs for the first time in many years.

Leo was a mixture of the new and the old. He tolerated some long hair and peacock plumage, and in the beginning the business of taking a man's money, of fining him, was avoided if possible. Both points went against tradition. But the tradition of long practices, even the day before a game, still held. So did emotional locker room speeches. He's an emotional man and it shows. Sometimes, when the pressure was heavy, we thought he had caved in. During the latter half of the 1970 season, when we were folding at an amazing rate, he got in the habit of raving in the meeting room before practice, and we'd spend the rest of the day trying to figure out what he had been yelling about.

And there are the Cahillisms. When Leo gets wound up, he talks in expressions and clichés. It isn't that some offensive or defensive manoeuvre won't work, but "that old dog won't hunt". A running play will "bust open like a suitcase", and there was the defensive back who was so short "he had to stand on two bricks to kick a duck in the ass". Then there was the warning about blowing an assignment or making some kind of error: "If you miss, just continue on out those gates, turn right, head for the lake and keep going till your hat floats".

And the conflicts. Leo felt a player opposing his viewpoint was opposing him. Occasionally there was some talk but little in the way of communication. Before the 1969 season, the Toronto veterans stayed away from the first few days of training camp trying to pressure the club into providing some kind of pay for all the time spent in training camp prior to the league season. During the "strike" Leo came out to talk to us. We made a great effort to let him know that this was the only action we had left to take against the front office after years of being ignored and we felt bad that he was caught in the middle. We were sure he understood why we were holding out, but that night the media carried stories that he felt we had put him down, and that in fact he didn't know if he wanted any of us back. When the incident ended a couple of days later, we had to solemnly file into his office, one by one, and dutifully answer "Yes" to the question, "Are you ready to do what's necessary in order to reach the Grey Cup?"

There have been other conflicts, some more open than others. And it always boils down to a matter of communication, sometimes nonexistent but always insufficient. The list includes names like Norm Stoneburgh, Bill Frank, Wally Gabler, Bobby Taylor, Mike Wadsworth, Tom Wilkinson, Don Jonas, and more. Some will quietly say, "No problem", and walk away because nice guys don't rock the boat. That's football's "Catch 22". You see, the ultimate goal in the sports system is sportsmanship. But the supreme test of sportsmanship is that when the sportsman gets screwed by the system, he accepts it humbly. The individual who protests, is of course, a bad sport.

One of the most interesting relationships within the club is that of the Head Coach to the General Manager. Only they know how it works, but it's fun to watch. And the results can cure you or kill you.

B.C. made people sit up and take notice before the 1971 season when Jackie Parker became General Manager and Eagle Keys Head Coach. They had worked well together as players, and Eagle Keys had an impressive coaching record in Saskatchewan. One of the things that impressed quarterback Tom Wilkinson most when he reported to the Lions was a statement by Eagle Keys that he intended to build a dynasty in Vancouver. Off their first year together and the recent recruiting, that's not such a bad bet.

I think the classic example relating to this point occurred in 1970. Montreal's new General Manager Red O'Quinn brought in Sam Etcheverry to coach the Alouettes. In their first year they transformed a last place team into Grey Cup champions. From the outhouse to the penthouse.

Then there is Toronto. In keeping with Argonaut tradition, John Barrow opened his tenure as General Manager in 1971 with an absurd welcoming address to the veterans. Its impossible to duplicate the emotional changes I went through as I sat there with 28 other men . . . . some the age, or nearly the age, of John Barrow . . . . . . and listened to him address the people he had been hired to deal with, reportedly because of his leadership qualities. John opened by stating he felt he was in a position to bridge the gap that exists between management and players, which in fact he was having just come from a 14 year career as a player. In the next breath he told us that, in as much as we represented the city of Toronto, we had an obligation to present a "respectable" appearance, and since he didn't feel long hair was respectable, many of those present would have to get haircuts. He quickly assured us, though, that the fact he wears a crew-cut had nothing to do with his decision. I sat there thinking: "This is 1971, this is a group of relatively intelligent people, and this really isn't happening". It was. A few minutes later he categorized everyone as a bunch of "overpaid losers". After that I kind of lost interest in our new leader. So much for bridging gaps.

35

B.C. Lions' Eagle Keys:
A dynasty in Vancouver?

Montreal's Sam Etcheverry:
Poise on the sidelines, a
Grey Cup his first year.

There are specific subjects I'm asked about more often than others, particularly by young people. I guess the very reason the questions are asked is because the subjects are studiously avoided by football. The system adopts an "ignore it and it will go away" attitude.

One of the subjects regards racism in football. What's it like for a black man?

A white man, by virtue of being white, can never know. But there are a couple of incidents that influenced me because they involved me directly or indirectly. In 1967 or 1968, Bob Taylor, an all-star defensive end from Winnipeg, came to Toronto in a trade. One of the first things he said was that he was looking forward to playing here because he'd heard Leo Cahill was "colour-blind". It was a tribute to Leo; but for the first time it made me aware that I've never had to include my colour in any consideration of where or for whom I wanted to play.

Less than a year later, I was asked by an agency to audition for the lead in a beer commercial because I was a football player. I declined so they asked me to recommend a teammate. I suggested Ed Harrington which put them in the embarrassing position of having to apologize, but the beer company wasn't interested in a black man for the lead.

Even without personal involvement, there are cold, hard, irrefutable facts that the "game" refuses to face, whether out of tradition, fear, or ignorance, I'm really not sure.

The most obvious example belongs in this section. Professional football has been played for approximately 75 years, and there is currently a total of 35 major teams. The number of head coaching jobs available in that period of time may be in the thousands, yet there has never been a black Head Coach in the history of pro football.

Yes, there is racism.

Ottawa's Jack Gotta
should have lots of joy in
the future. His Rough
Riders are getting tougher.

Winnipeg's Jim Spavital has put together the most potent offence in the C.F.L.

Dave Skrien: With George Reed and Ron Lancaster there shouldn't be a great deal to worry about.

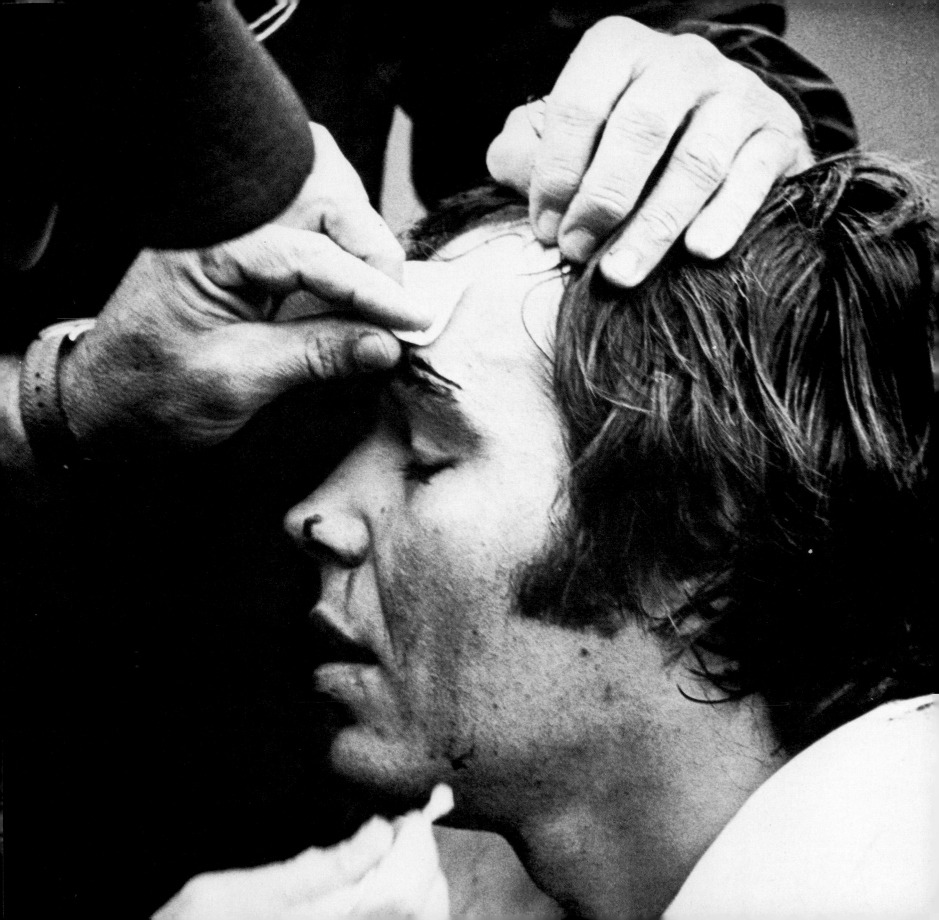

You've Got to Play Hurt

Chapter 3

It's easy to remember arriving in Toronto for the first time. I stepped off the plane on my 25th birthday, carrying just about everything I owned in two suitcases, and with a leg that had turned purple from hemorrhaging after I pulled a hamstring muscle in the B.C. Lions training camp. As far as football was concerned, I was at the end of the line.

In 1964 my first pro team, the Los Angeles Rams, let me go after a similar hamstring injury kept me sidelined throughout most of the training camp. Three thousand miles later I spent the remainder of the season on the taxi squad of the Pittsburgh Steelers and had to undergo the second of three knee operations just prior to the end of the season. I'd come those three thousand miles back to the West Coast to join the B.C. Lions in 1966 and tore the hamstring midway through the first practice. Now another three thousand miles and Toronto.

Within a few hours I met the man who gave me the chance to stay whole and play again. His name is Mert Prophet. He has been the trainer for the Toronto Argonauts for six of the past eight years and he is all those honourable things that sport is said to embody in a man.

Injuries are part of the game. That's a cliche, but in the idiom of the sport it's also indisputable fact. It joins two other popular cliches to cover the entire spectrum of injuries. Next comes "you've got to play hurt", then "you've got to live with the pain". After that they bury you.

Ironically, it takes an injury to make you realise just how total and absolute the indoctrination in sports can be. Because regardless of it severity, regardless of your value to the team, regardless of any and all circumstances, if an injury keeps you off the playing field, you automatically become one part "outsider". As long as you are unable to play, you cannot be part of "them". Incredible as it sounds, the feeling most strongly associated with injury is guilt.

One of the unwritten rules
of the game is never relax,
even after the whistle.
Gene Mack was hit from
the blind side after the
play and finished the game
on the sidelines.

It's drilled into a player from day one; an injury is not merely a physical weakness, it's a character weakness. That's why you've got to be "mentally tough", that's why you've got to "play hurt", that's why you've got to "live with the pain". It's macho. And it's the ultimate masculinity trip...transcending pain.

At the end of that first season, one game from the end of the schedule, we faced Ottawa in a home game. The Rough Riders' left defensive end was Billy Joe Booth, the best I've played against in Canada. Billy Joe kept his forearms taped, as do many defensive lineman, but it was such a heavy tape job I got the idea he had a baseball bat attached to each elbow.

Late in the third quarter he caught me above the face guard across the bridge of my nose and knocked the hell out of me. When the lights came back on, the only sensation I felt was pain. Mert was already there and it was obvious from the stains on my jersey and the towel in his hand that the bleeding was heavy. As we started off the field he would reach up with the towel to stop the flow of blood but I would just push it away. Finally I pushed it away and heroically mumbled something like, "I don't need it". He just shoved it back and said, "Yeah, but you're bleeding all over old Mert". I remember thinking at the time that that was not the right line!

One of the mysteries about football that holds people is the question of fear. Aren't you afraid of being hurt? Doesn't it frighten you to know you can be hit so hard? The answer is that on the field you become so detached from fear of being hurt that even injury to another player does not induce fear for yourself.

The one fear that I feel, and conversations with other players have taught me it's a common emotion, is the fear of not performing well, of not doing the job. But I've read comments by some great players that they always know that they can't be stopped, they just need the opportunity. I wonder if that might not be the single greatest difference between the so-called stars and the rest of us. Then again, maybe just being given the opportunity is the difference.

The morbid fascination occasionally shown regarding pain and injuries is one of the down trips in the sport. In a 1971 Montreal game, Mike Eben was hit hard making a diving catch at midfield. I was about 15 yards away and started over to him when he didn't get up, but Mert made the 30 yards from the sidelines before I got there. Mike was obviously hurt but there wasn't anything I could do, so I turned around to join the rest of the team in the offensive huddle. In the middle of the field, about 10 yards away, weaving around like a big, ugly vulture was a newspaper photographer snapping pictures. I started toward him with the thought of kicking him right out of the stadium, but I stopped when I realized he probably had the right to be out there and to profit from our blood. I'm sure the league has it written somewhere in the fine print of our contracts.

In all of sports nothing is more discouraging or frustrating than an injury. As I said before, if it's serious enough that you can't play you feel like an outsider. If you can play, odds are that you are only able to play at a percentage of your best. And the knowledge that you don't have complete control of your ability, that it's impaired to a certain degree by your injury, forces you to go one step further in your mind to try and even up.

The hardest determination to make on an injury is whether or not it is too serious for the man to play. The decision is made by the team Doctor and this is the rule of thumb: if the injury is such that no further damage can occur from continued playing, then you play. On some if not most teams the final decision is up to the coach, and there have been stories of men being put in a game despite being ruled out by the Doctor. I only know of one case first-hand, though.

Often a shot of pain killer evens things up. But in many cases, you have to play hurt. Saskatchewan quarterback Ron Lancaster played the 1970 season with an elbow so painful that at times he went the entire week between games unable to throw the ball. And he won the league's Most Valuable Player award.

In 1971 Jerry Keeling injured a shoulder and missed five or six games until he was able to come back and quarterback Calgary to a Grey Cup championship.

Also in 1971 Toronto's Joe Vijuk played nearly the whole season with a shoulder separation. I separated my shoulder in the final play-off game against Hamilton and played the Grey Cup game that way. At the same time Larry Brame was playing with a broken hand.

But the man who most amazes me, as well as just about everyone else in the league, is the man they say is referred to in Regina as Number One, Ed McQuarters. To come back and play after losing an eye takes more courage than I can even begin to understand.

I mentioned the use of painkillers, and I know that brings up questions about the use of other drugs in football. It's another subject studiously avoided by the system. I answer these questions in the street so I should be able to answer them here, although I'm a bit gun shy.

The first question always is, "Are drugs like pep pills or

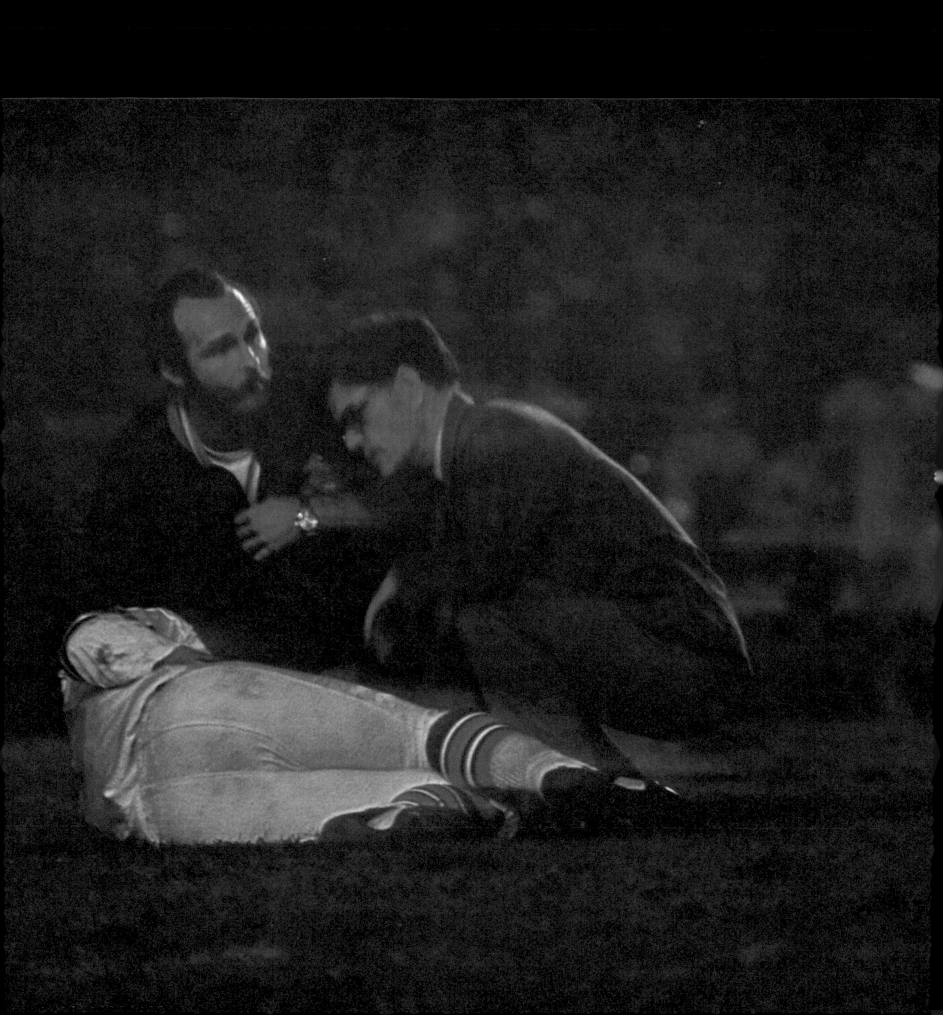

'bennies' used in football?" Yes, they've been used for a long time. That fact has been documented so many times in articles and books by athletes themselves that it always surprises me that I hear the question as often as I do.

Why are they used? Players take them to get an "edge" over the next guy. Or to catch up with the guy who is already taking them and therefore, theoretically, has that edge.

Do I use them? I tried them for a couple of games my first year in the league. Curiousity or stupidity, take your pick. They made me feel speeded up. I didn't like the feeling. It's an ugly sight to see a guy pop a handful and get so wound up he's barely coherent.

What's done about it? Nothing. It would be difficult to police because it's an individual matter, but no attempt is made in any case.

Why am I gun shy? In the winter I addressed a Toronto high school in a question and answer period. One of the questions involved the fact that athletes had written about the use of drugs in sports. Was it true? My answer, using some of the material above, took up maybe thirty seconds to a minute of that one hour session, and was in regard to only one of perhaps 100 questions. Yet the next day a newspaper article concerning only that single topic appeared under the headline, "Players Take Drugs Says Argo Captain". It was blown out of all proportion.

An acknowledgement of a violent game. The trainer attending this player has a great deal to do with how quickly and how well he will recover. One coach said he felt a good trainer was worth two wins over a season's schedule.

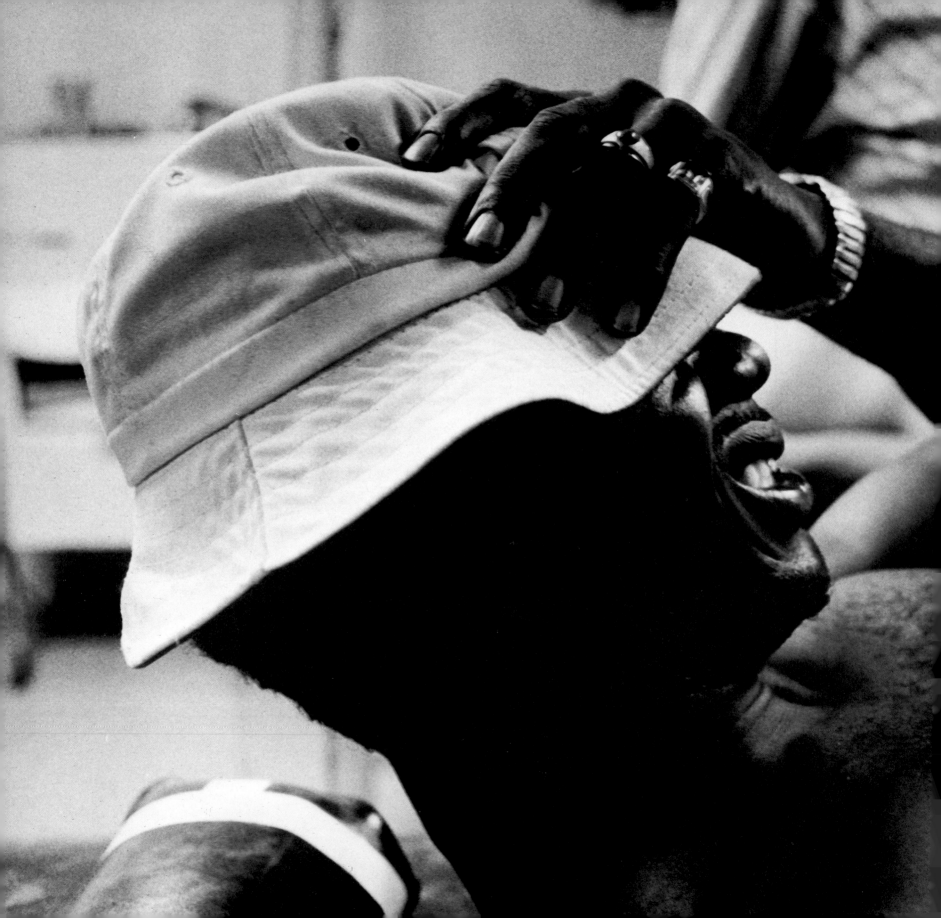

The length of a running back's career is as dependent on the condition of his knees as on any other single factor. Leon McQuay missed two games after exploratory surgery late in the 1971 season, then faced the same daily routine of taping for every workout that has claimed many others. The outstanding backs in recent Argonaut history have all had their careers influenced by knee injuries. Bill Symons was washed out of the N.F.L. and tried as a defensive back in Canada after knee surgery slowed him up. Since it's healed, he has become a thousand yard groundgainer. Dave Raimey initially lost a step after his knee injury, and has switched to a defensive cornerback.

Injuries, even few in number, can reduce a good team to mediocrity because of the limited rosters in the C.F.L. Montreal faded from Grey Cup champions to last place, not necessarily because of injuries, but they were a factor.

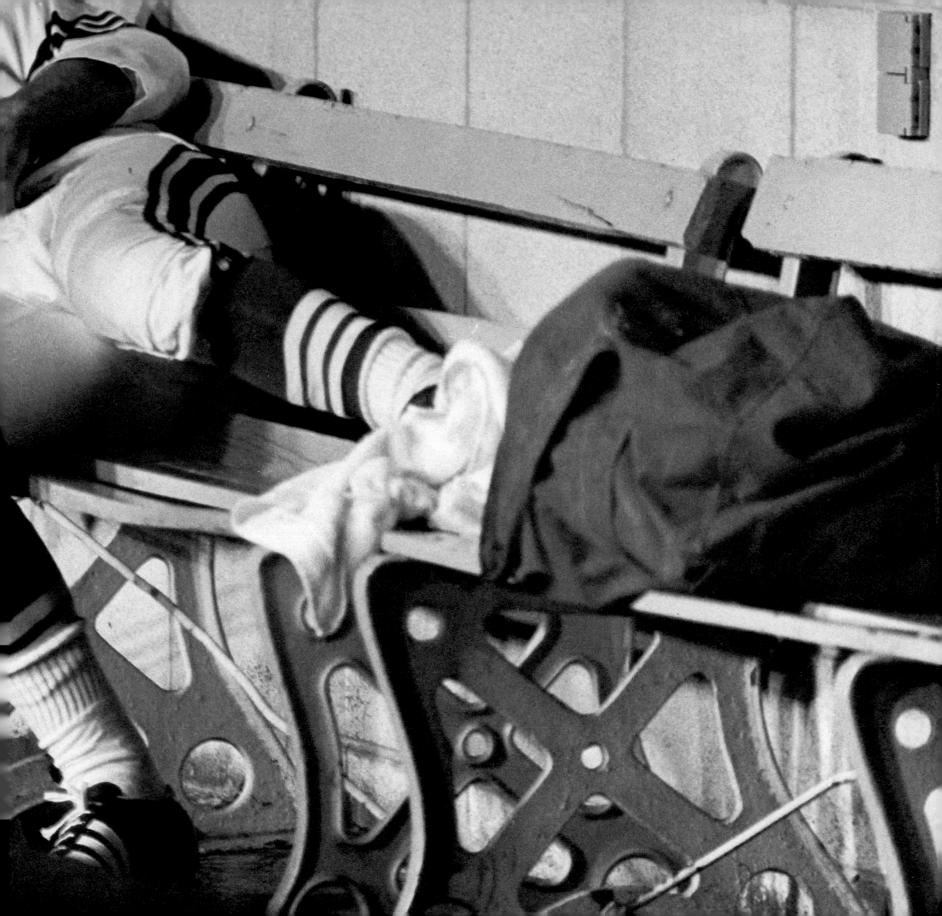

In the opinion of the officials, there was no infraction on this play. Late hitting is a judgment call, one not always shared by players. It's also the most dangerous offence in the game.

Dave Knechtal was the Eastern Conference rookie of the year in 1968. Then he missed the better part of three seasons, first with a broken leg, then knee surgery, and in this 1971 game a dislocated elbow.

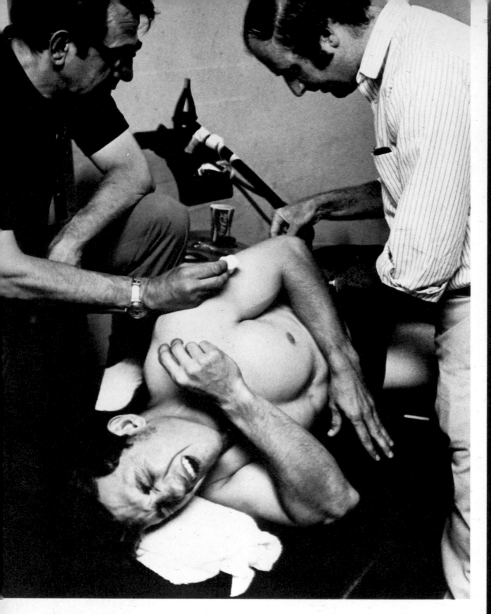

There are two people a player is committed to believe in because their decisions have a tremendous influence on his career. One is the trainer, the other is the team physician. It is the doctor's responsibility to decide if an injured player is capable of performing or if he might sustain further injury and must, therefore, be ruled out of a game. Dr. Grant Stewart administers an injection to Jim Tomlin, then stitches Harry Abofs following a game.

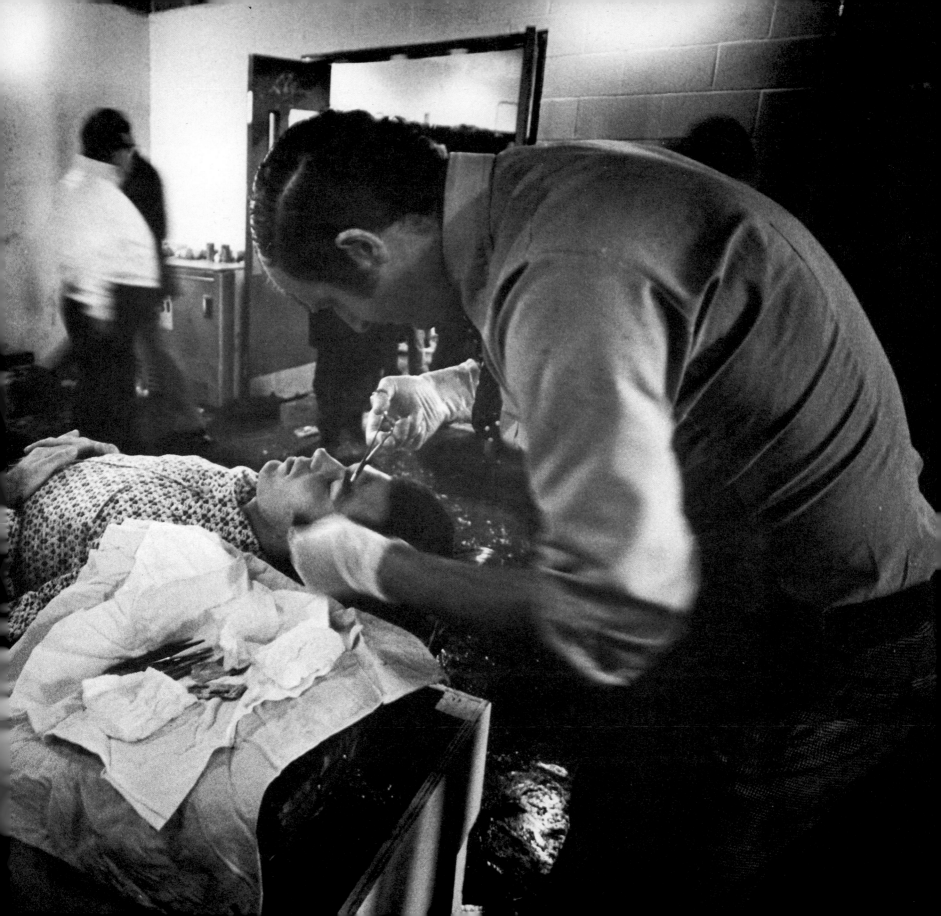

Joe Zuger quarterbacked Hamilton to Grey Cups in the 1960's, but his career may have come to an end on the C.N.E. running track. His shoulder was badly damaged in this final league game in 1971.

Hurry Up and Wait

Chapter 4

In 1965 after a Monday night game in Edmonton, the Toronto Argonauts left by plane to return home. All that is except all-star guard Ed Harrington. Ed had a fear of flying and instead travelled by train. He left Tuesday morning and arrived back in Toronto Thursday in time to drive to Hamilton for the game that night. As a direct result of this problem he was cut from the team not much later. Within three years, after conquering that fear, Ed returned to the C.F.L. and became an All Canadian defensive end.

Travelling provides the "hurry up and wait" aspect of football since you may be on the road for three days and spend ten or twelve hours on planes and buses just to play sixty minutes of football.

The regular season's schedule is set up so that a team covers all the cities in the league over a two season period. For example, one year the Argonauts may visit three western cities, the next year those three western teams come to us and the Argonauts travel to the two remaining western teams. A number of factors determine your outlook on a given road trip. Sometimes you dread it, sometimes you look forward to it. The city you're visiting, how well the team you are about to face is playing, whether it's a one game trip or two game trip, who you know at your destination—all these affect your outlook.

Of all these factors, I think the most important is the city itself. Generally speaking, there are three cities ballplayers look forward to visiting: Vancouver, Montreal, and Toronto.

These may seem like obvious choices simply because they happen to be the three largest. That's incidental to us. They rate because they have the most to offer in the way of ladies, entertainment, and various and sundry other diversions.

Now, my immediate reaction is to qualify the above as a bachelor's opinion and point out that these cities offer a wide variety of theatres and art galleries for the married men. But I'm afraid it would create a credibility gap from which we might never recover. There are, however, occasions when candidness is overruled by tact, and this is one of those occasions.

Road trips are essentially a long, tiring drag but there are some pretty humourous incidents. Unfortunately most of them involve the actions of married men on an outing away from family restrictions. (Here you'll have to accept the mathematical fact that the tremendous majority of pro players are married.) So I am somewhat limited to emphasizing the tedium involved; for the other stories you'll have to talk to the players yourself.

No, of course not, Madam! I am certainly not referring to your husband.

For an eastern team going West, Vancouver can make the difference between a good or bad trip. It's much easier to face that five hour plane trip when you know the B.C. brand of western hospitality awaits you.

There's always an element of surprise involved too. Dick Thornton met a Vancouver lady on our 1968 road trip and married her. I've always considered marriage to be something of a surprise.

I guess what it boils down to is that despite the pressure of a football game, B.C. is an enjoyable place to visit. It's one of those few places where you can honestly appreciate the beauty of a large city, a place where people enjoy being friendly. It's also the place where a player once got tanked up at the hotel after a game, charged into the coaches' suite to complain about curfew restrictions, then exited chuckling when he found the bosses were entertaining some ladies themselves.

Vancouver is also the spot where I learned an early lesson in the fine art of breaking curfew. The fact is I'm a good boy the night before a game. I always abide by curfew that night, not so much because I believe an early bedtime is beneficial as because I want to avoid any guilt feelings should we have a bad game the next day. But two nights before a game—that's different. I'm one of those people that just can't get to sleep early, so sometimes I like to get out for a late walk...or crawl as the case may be.

There's one simple law that governs breaking curfew; don't get caught. The basic format of the game....it has to be a game, otherwise how does a thirty-year-old man rationalize bed-checks and curfews...is this: curfew is an established time, usually 10:00 or 11:00 p.m. when a team official, normally a coach, tours the hotel from room to room making sure all the players are tucked in. Assuming everybody is smart enough to be present for bed-check, the activity begins when the coach departs. The key to a successful run

Dick Thornton, only two hours away from game time, on the team bus.

is in getting out and back in the hotel without being seen. Ironically I've never run into any teammates on my way out, but I've met quite a few on the return trip the next morning. Now some players can give you from memory the locations of rear exits, garage exits, and service elevators in major hotels across Canada. But so can some coaches. Also, there have been times when a club will actually post someone in the hotel lobby to keep an eye out for the bad guys.

The Vancouver lesson is beautiful for its simplicity. You eliminate the risk of being seen because you never leave the hotel. The people who were taking care of my insomnia checked into a room a few floors above the one on which the players were residing, so to join them, I went up rather than down. Two days later I played a brilliant game.

If you are wondering why all the effort to avoid detection, there are two reasons: emotional and monetary.

Emotional because your captors will drive you to the point of committing hari-kari. Any low life who would dare engage in such a dastardly act as sneaking out after curfew doesn't deserve to play football. I mean anyone who would let down his teammates, coaches, country and God like that just has to be punished. So they fine him. Which brings up the monetary angle.

One of the first documents issued to a player every year is a list of Training Rules that govern the individual throughout the season. In Toronto they are issued with the play book given in training camp. As a matter of fact, they make up page one. There are ten rules listed, plus a couple of inspirational suggestions like the final line, "**All dissenters will have a quick change of address!**" Two of those ten rules apply to the aforementioned topic, curfew and its cause. One of them states, "**Curfew is 11:00 p.m. at camp and on road trips unless otherwise notified. ($100 fine or suspension for violations.)**" The second reads, "**Fine or suspension for any unauthorized personnel in your room during camp or on road trips. ($100 first fine.)**" Guess who "unauthorized personnel" refers to. Anyway, detection under the circumstances referred to earlier, combining both the no-no's of these two rules, could mean either suspension or $200 in fines right off the top. At that rate I'd be playing football for free.

One of the most memorable "unauthorized personnel" stories happened a couple of years ago out West, in Calgary, I believe. We played the first game of a two game road trip in Winnipeg where one of our players met a member of the hotel staff and "imported" her to Calgary for the second game. Not long after we settled in, they got on the hotel elevator at the seventh floor, Leo Cahill got on at the sixth floor, I got on at the fifth floor, took one look and got off at the fourth. I didn't hear any more about it, but I never saw her again. He's no longer with the club either. But he's an all-pro on another C.F.L. team.

For those who may be curious about other training rules, here are a few more.

"You must be on time for all team functions. Latecomers will be fined. ($50 first fine.)"
That rule was somewhat flexible. We had one guy who tended to be a little late . . . . like a day or two . . . . and never got fined a nickel.

"We do not encourage drinking and will legislate against drunkenness. A fine will be imposed on anyone seen in a bar 48 hours prior to a game. ($100 first fine.)"
We called this our "Four-Ta-Eight" rule, as in "Stay out of the bar from four ta eight". These happen to be the hours we work out.

"Smoking will be allowed only in the dressing room."

"Any gambling is prohibited. On road trips, think football."
Amen!

Somehow over the past few years our western road trips have managed to get tied in with race tracks. Dick Thornton and I like to spend some time handicapping and we get the opportunity out West.

The track in Vancouver is right across the P.N.E. grounds from Empire Stadium and provides us with a serious opportunity to lose money. But our favorite track is in Edmonton. We usually manage to watch the trotters at least one night while we're there. The quality isn't much but the laughs are great. In 1971 we actually came home money ahead after a photo finish between a horse that looked like a mutt and another that resembled a groundhog. We won with the groundhog. The funny thing about it was we beat Edmonton in a photo finish the next night when on the last play of the game, they missed a field goal attempt, which would have beat us.

The track gets us in Regina too. That's where the practice field is located, on the infield of a track.

Western players coming East have somewhat of an advantage in that two of the four cities have a great deal to offer. But it can be negated by the fact that a western team may have to play two games with only one day's rest in between.

Montreal is magic. Since I first arrived in Canada, I've heard more players talk about that city than any other. When we get to Montreal, players head out of the hotel with a purpose and, in most cases, with a destination. It's a first class city in direct contrast to its earlier football facilities.

Before they moved to the Autostade, the Alouettes used Molson Stadium as a home field. The dressing room facilities were so bad we used to suit-up in our hotel rooms before the game, bus to the stadium then bus back and shower at the hotel afterwards.

Toronto holds a great deal of interest too. I think the primary reason is because so many players on visiting teams were with the Argos at one time and it is much like a homecoming.

Hamilton has a lot of STELCO signs.

To ease the problem of travelling a bit, airlines have taken to seating teams before they board any remaining passengers.

At first I thought the move was designed strictly to benefit the club. Later I was told by airline personnel that there is a more practical explanation. We are always seated in the middle of the plane to balance the load. I think they're afraid that if we all crowd in front or back, we'd be flying vertically instead of horizontally, and it makes them nervous. I know it makes me nervous. Since I found that out I panic at the thought of the whole club getting up at once to visit the washroom.

One of the undeniable pleasures of flying is the opportunity to make new friends, hopefully among the stewardesses, but the possibilities are reduced due to the circumstances. Baby-sitting a return flight after a game is an unenviable job to say the least. A group of men too large for the facilities and as often as not in some degree of pain can be a little demanding.

One of the first C.F.L. "folk-tales" I heard on entering the league involved an Ottawa team celebrating on a return flight that got so belligerent they stuffed the stewardesses in the overhead rack for the duration of the trip.

Once we're on board we are easily categorized as card players, readers, or sleepers. I started out as a reader, moved up to card playing, then eventually found that as soon as I sat down I went out like a light. It's like a disease. One year we boarded a flight to Ottawa, and my eyes closed the moment I sat down. I half woke up when I heard a voice on the public address system talking about a firewarning or something having to do with a fire. I knew that was no time to be a few thousand feet in the air, and I panicked when Charlie Bray grabbed his hat and announced he was leaving. When I finally bothered to check out the window, I found we were parked at the end of the runway at the Toronto airport.

Zenon Andrusyshyn and
Jim Corrigal: Squabble over
Midwest Honkers!

The Cast

Chapter 5

Pro football holds a strange fascination for people. It's done a beautiful job of promoting itself. The feeling I get from fans and the public in general is that it is the epitome of sport, the be all and end all.

That's where professional football and I don't see things quite the same. It's a personal philosophy, but I think the minute a sport comes to depend solely on selling tickets for its existence, the basic values are changed, primarily the value given to winning. I'm sure most people who care are aware that it's a pretty cold-blooded business. It keeps its place in society because it's entertainment. For the same basic reason people pay exorbitant prices to see any type of theatre, they pay exhorbitant prices to see pro football. They want to be entertained.

When we talk about entertainment, I think it is generally accepted that a brilliant performance by the lead actors will go a long way towards selling tickets and ensuring success. In football we call them superstars.

We have our cast of stars in the C.F.L. but it's undergoing some extensive changes. Now folklore emphasizes the 1950's with tales of Jackie Parker, Normie Kwong, Johnny Bright, Dick Shatto, Hal Patterson, Sam Etcheverry, Leo Lewis, Tex Coulter, Cookie Gilchrist, the list growing and changing according to the preferences of the speaker.

The 60's are still too recent, but some of those names are long enough gone that they seem to melt into the first group. George Dixon, Tobin Rote, Joe Kapp, Willie Fleming, Eagle Day, Don Luzzi, Kenny Ploen, even players as recent as Russ Jackson, Dave Mann and Ronnie Stewart for some just getting turned on to the game. The current stars with some exceptions, are at the end of their careers. In the next couple of years, a new generation of football fans will have to hear second-hand about legends like Marv Luster, Garney Henley, Dick Thornton, George Reed, Bobby Taylor, Ron Lancaster,

Calgary's Granville Liggins: The quickest offensive lineman in Canadian football.

Dave Raimey, Angelo Mosca, Tommy Joe Coffey, Ken Sugarman, Wayne Harris, Herm Harrison, Bill Frank; again make your own list.

The 70's start a new era with two distinct characteristics. First, the new breed are Americans commanding unprecedented bankrolls and matching publicity. Second, many of the Deans of the era are Canadian.

The league has a new measuring stick to wave—the N.F.L. draft. Actually, it's been waved in the past, but never with the authority or fanfare it receives today. In 1971 the league scored its initial N.F.L. first-round draft selection. Tim Anderson chose Toronto over San Francisco. The same year three other early round draft picks signed with Toronto and a few more made their way into the league with other clubs. Add to that the one or two other players who annually come up here before finishing their U.S. college eligibility and are given honorary "first round pick had he stayed" status, and you can understand the enthusiasm. In the winter of 1972, three U.S. All America stars had signed with the C.F.L. and it looked like more might come. The new signings have created some great rumours about incredible salaries and contracts. They have a lot of people in the league salivating. They also have a lot of people confused, particularly those perennial all star players who are still trying to figure out what more they have to do to earn that kind of contract.

The new era is bringing with it another break in football tradition. The days of the monosyllabic moron are gone. The people coming to pro ball aren't very tolerant of commands to wear crew cuts and confine off-the-field activities to nothing more radical than a beer with the boys. Whether they do or not isn't important. They demand the choice be their own, not dictated to them. Nor are a lot of them afraid to criticize the weaknesses in the pro sports system. And they know the possible consequences.

Ironically, these are the very points that may give pro football its greatest strength. The game has to appeal to the new, young fan in order to grow and maintain its popularity. And the young are finding it easier to identify with some of the new people than with the old sterotype.

When I'm reflecting on players I've faced in the league, there are certain names that always return. It surprised me one day to suddenly realize the majority of these people came from one team, the Ottawa Rough Riders.

A tight end has personal battles with three different defensive positions. He blocks a great deal of time on defensive ends, blocks and faces some pass coverage from outside linebackers, and has a defensive safety in coverage the rest of the time.

The best defensive player I faced in Canada was Billy Joe Booth. He was consistently the smartest and quickest defensive end in the league. Two others that stood out were Bob Taylor when he was in Winnipeg and Dick Suderman in Calgary. In 1971, another Rough Rider joined my list and from the few times I faced him he may be the strongest I've played against yet. His name is Tom Laputka.

Among outside linebackers, the most consistent has been Gerry Campbell. Again a very smart football player, never out of position, and also very quick. Two others are Hamilton's Mike Blum and Montreal's Mark Kosmos. They rely more on size and strength.

Among defensive backs, you know there's one name you're always going to hear: Garney Henley. I think he knows and understands defensive football better than any man in the game. One of the reasons I hoped to be used more as a pass receiver was to become enough of a threat that I would face him more often, just for the opportunity to challenge the best there is.

One other back sticks out in my mind, but I didn't face him in game situations. I used to work after practice against Chip Barrett because I found that, aside from Garney Henley, he was the hardest pass defender to beat. I've never really been able to use in a game what I developed in practice, but I got pretty good at kidding myself that the chance would come.

The C.F.L. has had its share of characters, people that blend madness with ability. For instance, it seems like every day I come across somebody with a new story about a Cookie Gilchrist business venture that went belly up.

Joe Kapp is one of those magic players that people say is "colourful". He is, and has been for a very long time. Before he came to Canada he was the quarterback who took the University of California Golden Bears to a Pacific Coast Championship and the 1959 Rose Bowl. At the same time I was in my last year of high school 50 miles away. I used to take the bus up the coast to Berkeley on Saturdays and usher at the Cal home games so I could get in free to see him play. In those days he received the greatest amount of publicity as a runner because Cal used a Split-T offence in which the quarterback had the option to run on most plays. Joe Kapp was already a legend, at least in the San Francisco Bay area, and the greatest moment of my life to that point came when the California coaching staff offered me an athletic scholarship to play at Cal and be "the next Joe Kapp". I had been a single-wing tailback in football my senior year and decided instead to go to one of the few remaining major colleges playing single wing football, UCLA. That really tore up my parents because they were also Joe Kapp fans. In fact the moment they remember best about the 1971 Grey Cup they saw twelve years later occurred when Joe happened to walk by after the game and said hello.

There are two players whom I've known and watched personally in 17 years of football who, in terms of effort, emotion, unselfishness, and dignity, have given the game of football more than football will ever be able to repay. Joe Kapp is one, Marv Luster is the other.

In the seven seasons since I arrived, the resident madman has been Bobby Taylor. An unbelievable competitor on the field, he spends the rest of his time introducing reality to fantasy-land. The more boring, redundant or unnecessary the occasion, the more energetic and efficient is Bobby Taylor. And there are a lot of those occasions.

Bobby came to Toronto with Pete Manning in a trade from Calgary. They were close friends, and neither was prone to excessive sentiment. When I arrived wearing long hair (the hairline still hadn't been broken at that time) Pete turned to his friend and said, "Who is that?" Bobby's answer was, "You mean what is that?"

Pete later used a line in describing Bobby which is an all-time classic: "I didn't say he was ugly. I said his head wore out two bodies".

Following a game near the end of that first season, I needed seven stitches after a fore-arm had re-arranged my nose and by the time I got back from the hospital my face was black and blue and both eyes were slits because of the swelling. Bobby took one look and said, "Your face looks better".

Toronto has a magnetic attraction for qualified characters. Richard "Tricky Dick" Thornton ruled in Winnipeg until a disastrous season induced a trade to Toronto. Even during hard times he refused to concede an inch. About mid-season of his last year there as a defensive back, he switched football numbers for a change of luck. He doubled his previous number from 14 to 28 because he was "going to be twice as good". In his first game as number 28 he got beat for a touchdown and Winnipeg lost 7-3. His parting shot has already become a folklore staple. Asked what it was he liked best about Winnipeg, Dick answered, "The road leading out".

Mike Eben made the list before he even entered pro ball by

simply refusing to join the club that had drafted him from college. The 1968 season was under way before B.C. finally gave up and traded Mike to Toronto. He added a footnote to intra-league relations by being "loaned" to Edmonton for the 1970 season.

Mike is the Argonaut's absent-minded professor. He teaches at a university while studying for his Ph.D. and at times he gives the appearance of absolute obliviousness to his surroundings. We were at the airport leaving on a road trip to Montreal and were told to board the aircraft. As the team made a right turn, Mike drifted left and sat waiting patiently in an empty plane that was eventually destined for some place like South America. A stewardess finally guided him back to reality.

In 1971 two new dimensions were added to the list of super-stars. They were nearly extremes in relation to each other.

Leon McQuay brought with him perhaps the greatest degree of natural running ability in football today, regardless of league or country. It's all bound up in a quiet, reserved loner. People demand to know more—it's an obligation of sorts that a "star" assumes. But that's all he wanted known his first year.

At the same time, there was another new arrival from what I once heard described as the world's leading manufacturer of football players, Notre Dame. Joe Theismann is charisma. Like Leon McQuay, Joe has unlimited talent. He also has that rare ability to excite fans whatever the circumstances, to generate enthusiasm in a situation that would normally induce sleep. He is, in short, a natural showman, the kind of personality that P.T. Barnum would make room for. His personality is reflected in his style of play. His is undisciplined, go-for-broke football. He likes to throw the ball, "the long bomb" to use a cliche, and loves to run. I think he could easily make it as a halfback if he wanted.

One of Joe's strongest allies in his first year was the element of surprise. In a sense, it worked against him, too. Opposing defences were never sure of where to locate him, but neither were some of the people on his side. When I was running pass patterns, I never really expected to find Joe throwing from the spot where the playbook said he would be. Usually, the first thing I'd see was a bunch of defensive linemen chasing someone, and that would point me to Joe. From thirty yards downfield, it was like watching a scene out of the fox and the hounds.

At times it was a necessary manoeuvre because there was a breakdown in the pass protection. But often it was simply a matter of Joe relying on his running ability rather than waiting for the pattern to develop or the receiver to break open.

Through much of 1971 we used an alternating quarterback system with Joe and Greg Barton. Their situation dominated football coverage early in the year, so after a while we used to refer to practice as "the Greg and Joe show".

They could pass for brothers physically, but they are different personalities with different styles of play. Greg is low-keyed, relatively disciplined in his action, and quarterbacks much the same way. He prefers to establish an offensive pattern, to find a strength to go with or a weakness to work on. He learned discipline through his indoctrination into pro ball in the States.

Our system worked against Greg in 1971. It's impossible to establish any sort of pattern when you have only one series of downs to work with before giving way to another quarterback. A grab-bag offence favoured Joe because it allowed him to use his extensive ability better with fewer restrictions. Even though it was accidental, the end result was that Greg got the short end of the stick.

The working relationship between Joe and Greg is somewhat unique. The natural desire of a man who has a great deal of ambition, a great deal of talent, and who has already tasted a degree of success is to reach the top of his field. These characteristics just about define both men. Yet, here they are in a situation where only one will get that opportunity and the other will be relegated to being a reserve on his own team. They made it through the first year without any crisis because of a combination of factors, the most important being Leo Cahill's decision to alternate quarterbacks regardless of the situation. A broken finger that sidelined Greg for the last part of the season also forestalled any problems developing. But just how long two very talented and very competitive men can last under those circumstances remains to be seen. For all the dialogue you hear about living with a situation "for the good of the team", I never met a player worth a damn who felt he was doing the team any good by sitting on the bench.

Another question I often hear is, "Will so and so stay in the C.F.L.?" In Joe's case, challenges are a way of life and I think the odds are at least even that he'll try the N.F.L. someday. Ask me again in about two years. If he waits until 1976 or so, he may be on an N.F.L. team and still be in Toronto.

I mentioned earlier that American imports have been predominant among the new arrivals, both in salary and publicity. Jim Corrigall broke this string three years ago and is now one of those Canadian "Deans."

Jim came out of Kent State as the most heralded Canadian to

play U.S. college football. He came home to Toronto although a second-round draft choice in the N.F.L. and is now an All Canadian defensive end. The first time he walked into camp someone said, "Look at that big country boy", and he's been "Country" ever since.

There is a long list of Canadians at or near the top of their position. Contrary to popular belief they are there because they are the best athletes, not because of nationality.

For example, Dick Suderman rates with Jim Corrigall among the top four defensive ends even though he sat out the 1970 season.

Jim Young and Mike Eben are two of the league's best receivers, but Terry Evanshen is still on top of the list. He has all the ingredients of the perfect receiver, except for the unusual height looked for today. His is an exceptional blend of quickness, speed, hands, and football "smarts". Terry holds the record for the greatest number of passes ever caught in one year in the C.F.L. He set the record of 96 receptions in Calgary, then played out the club's option to try for big money either here or in the States. The general concensus of opinion was that he would never get it because he was Canadian, which precluded his having the ability. He got his contract in Montreal, and proved that it doesn't make any difference what he is because he does have the ability. He also proved the value of another consideration—confidence.

Mike Eben is a fraction behind Terry in quickness, speed, and experience and he still has to overcome one major fault. While he has the "hands", the ability to catch a pass to match any receiver in the game, he concentrates so totally on receiving the ball that he often gives up advancing it after the catch by diving or falling for passes which he could have caught while maintaining his balance.

One of my favourite stories in the game involves Bob Swift. Eight years ago as a running back, he gained over 1,000 yards. Now he's an All Canadian centre. The other centres to make all star in the past few years are also Canadians, among them Paul Desjardins and Basil Bark.

And, if he stays healthy, I think the best tight end over the next few years will be Peter Dalla Riva.

Winnipeg's Jim Thorpe: The
C.F.L.'s leading receiver
in 1971.

Montreal's Steve Smear:
Second only to Wayne
Harris among middle
linebackers.

**Toronto's Tommy Bland:
Time ran out.**

**Toronto's Jim Stillwagon:
The best defensive lineman
in the league.**

Hamilton's Garney Henley: It's all been said. There has never been a better athlete in the game.

B.C.'s Greg Findlay: The boss of the Lion's defence.

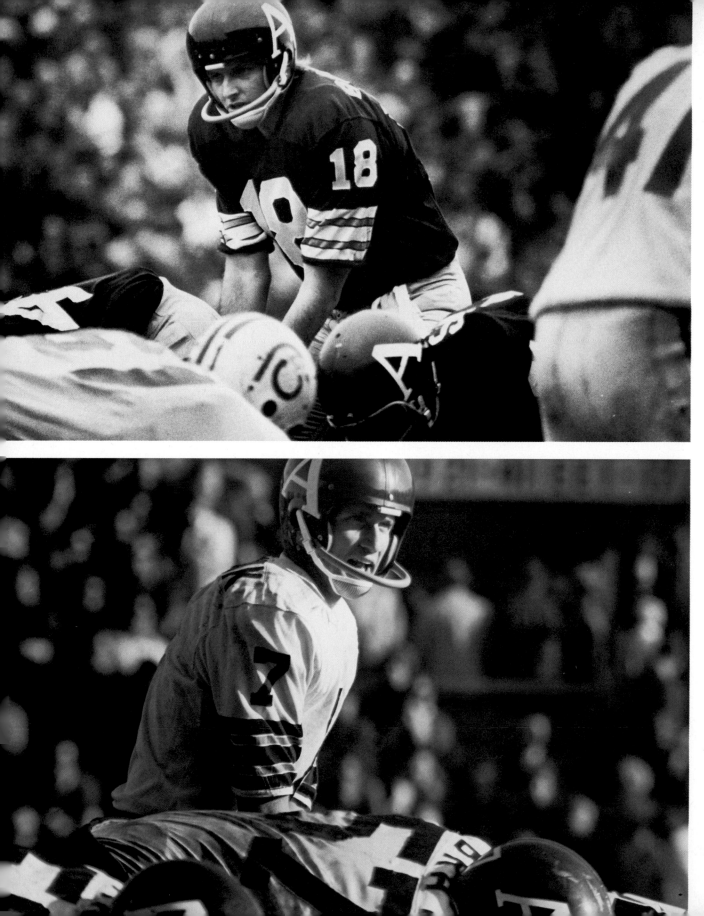

Hamilton's Angelo Mosca:
The quarterback's nemesis.

Toronto's Greg Barton and
Joe Theismann: The
quarterbacks.

87

Calgary's Rudy Linterman: The "unknown" back in the Grey Cup backfield.

Montreal's John Carlos: A world champion sprinter trying to make it work in a different game.

Hamilton's Wally Gabler:
A potential superstar among
quarterbacks.

B.C.'s Ken Sugarman:
A perennial all-star, the
only lineman left from the
Lion's glory days.

Saskatchewan's Ron Lancaster: The league's most valuable player in 1970.

Ottawa's Marshall Shirk: The constant factor in the C.F.L.'s best defensive line for nearly a decade.

Ottawa's Gerry Campbell: The toughest outside linebacker I faced in the league.

Montreal's Terry Evanshen: As near as you can get to the perfect receiver.

Toronto's Gene Mack:
Close to the top among
outside linebackers in his
first year.

96

There's an expression used in football for a hard, tough tackle. It's called "sticking". Marv Luster is and has been the hardest hitting defensive back in Canada for eight years. His teammates nicknamed him "Stickman".

Toronto's Leon McQuay: Perhaps the best running back in football.

Hamilton's Gary Inskeep: In keeping with the Hamilton tradition of big, tough linemen.

Saskatchewan's Ed McQuarters was considered through with football after an off-season injury. He missed less than half a season and on this night returned to a standing ovation.

Calgary's John Atamian:
A member of the offensive
line that gave the Stampeders a running attack
capable of winning a Grey
Cup.

In 1971, his first year as a defensive halfback, Dave Raimey intercepted four passes in league play even though he has trouble raising his arms above his head because of numerous shoulder operations.

(Clockwise) B.C.'s Jim Young, the league's out-standing Canadian in 1970. John Williams, possibly the best cornerback against the run in Canada. Bill Symons, the only Argonaut to ever rush for 1,000 yards or win the Most Valuable Player award. Ottawa's Rudy Sims and Montreal's Gord Judges, two young players at the strongest position in the league, defensive tackle.

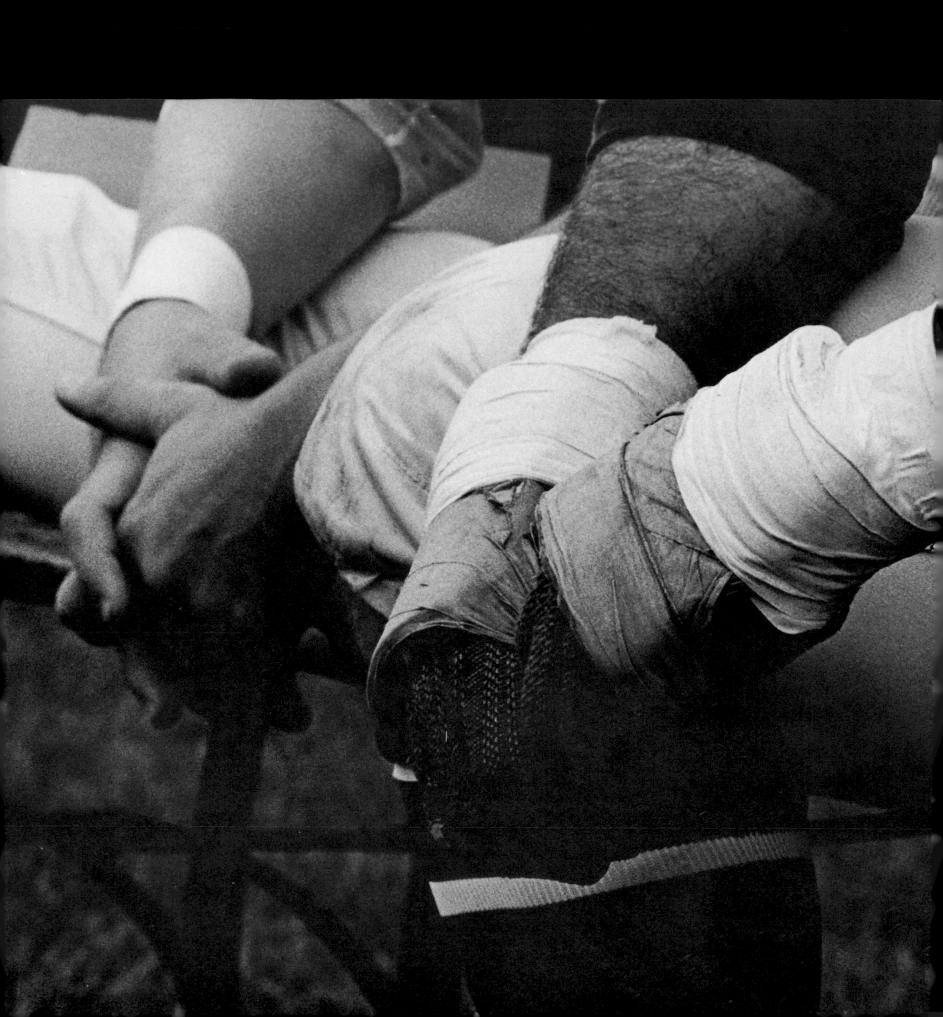

Part 2

For Sixty Minutes

Chapter 6

In 1964 with the Los Angeles Rams, I took my place in an offensive huddle for the first time as a pro. When I broke from the huddle and started up to the line, the first thing I saw was Deacon Jones, 6'6", 260 pounds, then Merlin Olsen, 6'5", 270 pounds, Roosevelt Grier, 6'5", 300 pounds, and Lamar Lundy, 6'6", 260 pounds. Uh oh!

Everyone has his own idea about what decides the outcome of a ball game. I've heard it credited to one player, or one coach, or dedication, or desire, even clean living as in "God was on our side". That's probably the reason it's such an interesting subject. So many people, most of them extremely knowledgeable and intelligent, can come to so many different conclusions.

Obviously there isn't any one answer. But the two factors that I think influence a game more than any other . . . . be it personnel, management, strategy, or conditioning . . . are emotions and chance.

They are the intangibles, the factors you can't arrange to suit your needs. The others you can pretty well control. Personnel and management are hand-picked, strategy is pre-determined, conditioning is an established fact, and on a professional level there isn't a tremendous variance among teams regarding factors like personnel or conditioning. So it comes down to emotion and chance.

The emotional aspect of the game is important for reasons other than its influence on the final outcome. It is the first consideration in becoming a football player, more accurately, in remaining a football player. Because when all is said and done, you can't do what is asked of a player unless you love the game.

I've never been able to believe the amount of abuse officials take during the course of a ballgame, particularly from the sidelines. If I were a ref, it wouldn't be for long. In 1971, as offensive captain, it was my job to discuss penalties that occurred on the field. So I had a chance to practice my preaching and said very little. The officials were so happy they gave me the Jeff Russell Memorial Award for it. I've gotten over the initial surprise I received when in going over the films after a "poorly officiated" game I invariably found that most of the calls were correct. The only legitimate complaint I heard was not in regard to the calls that were made, but the calls that were not made, particularly in dangerous penalties like piling on or late hitting. Even on the field, the best way to find out the kind of infraction involved is to watch the referee's signal. On the right is the indication of an illegal substitution. (I had to look it up in the program.)

For sixty minutes, from kick-off to final gun, there isn't anything else in the world. There is just the power of doing, of physical involvement, of willing yourself to overcome fatigue and sometimes pain, of matching your ability with that of another man equally as intense, and best of all, the beautiful satisfaction of achievement. It is an indictment on our society that we have taken away that satisfaction from so many people by equating achievement to winning.

We've all heard those stories of the coach whose locker room oratory sends a team crashing through walls on an invincible march to victory. They are pretty much just that......stories. On the day of a game, a man's emotional pitch will be determined more by his wife's health than by a plea to "win one for the Gipper".

Another emotional factor that influences the final outcome is the mass vibrations of a stadium full of people. That's why bookies give from three to six points to the home team when assessing a game. 33,000 people pouring down belief can inspire an individual.

The chance factor is expressed in a number of ways. Most people refer to it as luck, either good or bad. Statisticians refer to it in terms of "turnovers", those occasions when you turn the ball over to your opponent or he to you. Still others call it "the breaks", and chance also gave rise to the most obnoxious cliche of all, "that's the way the old ball bounces".

Reporters and sportscasters talk about "momentum". Basically they're referring to one team having the upper hand, and that is a direct result of turnovers or breaks or whatever. There are a lot of games that are won by the team that's not supposed to. In 1971 we were in Edmonton and favoured to win, but they played us even most of the time and outplayed us the rest of the time. Going into the last couple of minutes they had the ball and a five point lead. In all honesty Edmonton should have won that game. But we got a break ...Dave Raimey intercepted a pass on a play that probably shouldn't have been called...and we scored with about thirty seconds left. We got another break when Dave Cutler missed on a field goal try from half way around the world by six inches. Had it been good, we'd have lost by a point!

Our '71 season was a story of breaks or luck. We were able to face the West's two strongest teams on our own field, as well as catching them on the second game of their road trips. In both cases they played without a key player. Ed McQuarters hadn't returned to football yet, and Calgary played without their number one quarterback, Jerry Keeling. We beat them without Jerry, but when he came back Calgary beat us when it really mattered, in the Grey Cup.

Our early season strength was the fact we had such imposing individual talent. There was always someone to make a big play and put us in front. In our first Montreal game we had four different men go 75 yards or more on a single play. But offensively we rarely functioned with consistency, and defence become our strength over the last half of the year, topped by a fantastic performance in the Grey Cup.

Part of the great football mystique involves strategy. It's an ever-changing factor because your opponent actually dictates your choice of offence and defence by virtue of his weaknesses.

Most teams draw up a "game plan" for each opponent. Basically that means selecting those plays from the over-all offence which will work best against your opponents' anticipated defences and concentrating on your defensive set(s) best suited for stopping your opponents' offensive strength.

The material to draw from is extensive. For instance the Argos may initiate from as many as twelve different offensive formations (doubled in as much as they may usually be turned around either left or right) and make use of 20 to 25 basic running plays as well as screens, draws, and about 14 play action passes and drop back passes employing a dozen different pass patterns run by any one of six different pass receivers. The final game plan may reduce the numbers to perhaps six or eight running plays, a couple of screens and draws, and a half-dozen passes. But the multiples are still numerous.

For example, an off-tackle play might originate from one of six different formations, and the only thing remaining constant would be the hole through which the ball is to be carried. In one formation a setback might carry the ball, in another the slotback. Both the tackle and end might be blocking at the point initially, but a change of formation could split the end and a back would take over his blocking responsibilities.

If that's not enough to keep you thinking, defences change the blocking pattern for a given play. Not only might you run the same play from four separate formations, but running it against four different defences could change the blocking pattern each time.

Often the greatest drama in football is the battle of minds between the quarterbacks and their defensive counterparts, men like Wayne Harris, Garney Henley and Marv Luster. In a game where the breaks are fairly equal, those battles between individuals make the difference.

The job of calling defensive signals usually goes to the middle linebacker. A consistent exception since I've been in the league is Marv Luster

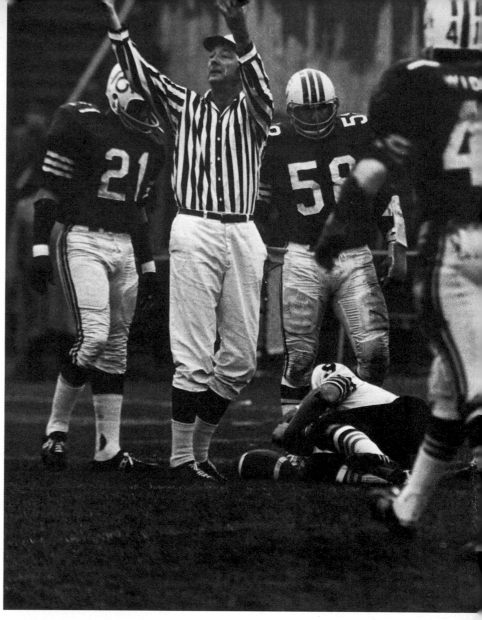

We talk about chance, of
football being a game
of breaks. A fumble is in-
excusable because it can
turn a game around. A loose
ball up for grabs can negate
an afternoon's work, as on
the left. Yet even though
Mike Eben was hit so
hard making a diving catch
of a pass that he had to
be carried from the field
and did not play again for
over a month, he still
held on to the ball for a
completion.

who works from a rover position, a job which allows him more freedom than any other defensive spot.

Among middle linebackers, there are two who have stood out over the past six years, Wayne Harris and Ken Lehmann. It was Ken backing Billy Joe Booth and Marshall Shirk that gave Ottawa the East's best defence and three Grey Cup starts in the late sixties.

Three straight years, 1967-68-69, Toronto faced Ottawa in the Eastern play-offs. Each year one game was played in Ottawa at Lansdowne Park. Each year we got killed, and each year there was a tinge of weirdness to the whole show.

1967 was the first time in quite a while that Toronto had made it to the play-offs. By finishing third we qualified for the semi-finals and took off for Ottawa to get our annual bombing from Russ Jackson.

The league rules regarding imports at the time stipulated only 13 of the 14 men could suit up for a game. The fourteenth man was called the "designated import". Well, it was a cold, wet, miserable day and our designated import brought along a flask to try and keep from freezing to death behind the bench. I figured out what was happening at half time because while the rest of us were trying to get warm and quit shaking, he had a nice bloom to his cheeks. Another player figured it out too and sampled the anti-freeze in the flask. I had trouble rationalising the whole thing then, but reflecting on it now after being nearly frozen to death and beaten by about 100 points, I'm glad someone got out of it without a great deal of pain.

In 1969 we faced Ottawa in the Conference finals for the Grey Cup spot. That brought about the worst mismatch I've ever had the misfortune to be involved in. The opening game of the two game total-point series was played in Toronto and ended with the Argos eight points ahead. The following Saturday we went to Ottawa to finish the series. Even considering our lead at the time we made one serious mistake. We should never have showed up.

It is the only time I can honestly say that game conditions were such that it was pointless to continue. The weather had been extremely cold for some time and Lansdowne Park was frozen solid. At game time the temperature was reported as 17° above but it felt like 50° below.

In preparation the Argos had come up with various cleats and even a new soccer shoe to use on the frozen turf. The fact was that any kind of cleat was the wrong cleat. If anything, it was necessary to wear a flat shoe that gave the greatest amount of contact on the ice surface. Ironically, the club had been unable to find any shoes to fit me (I wear a rather petite size 14 EEEE) and the only thing that I could come up with was a pair of canvas gym shoes. The end result was that I had better traction than anyone else in our club and it was lousy.

Ottawa showed up in broomball shoes which, in retrospect, certainly seems reasonable enough. The Rough Riders were in fact a better team than the Argos, having beaten us three out of four games that year, but they weren't so much better that they could beat us by 29 points, hold us to just one field goal and 32 yards total offence in the game, tying a C.F.L. record for least yards gained. Yet that is exactly what happened. It looked like opening night at the Ice Follies. Ottawa was the beautiful star and we were the clowns.

The most vivid recollection in my mind is a play which occurred early in the game. Deep in our own territory, we were forced to punt....again. Dave Mann was kicking and got off a fairly long kick, the kind a punt returner has plenty of time to catch. As one of the ends in coverage, I started down the field working up a full head of steam. Just as the returner fielded the ball I put on the brakes to check myself in order to respond in whichever direction he would move. Unfortunately, there were no brakes. I took off like I was on skis and just slid right on by the punt return man. To this day I swear he waved at me as I went by.

Shoes have become a new status symbol in football. Years ago there was only one kind of football shoe, the black high-top. Eventually low-tops became popular with runners and receivers and are now worn by everyone with the exception of an occasional lineman.

The big change came with the introduction of the white shoe. It has become the mark of the superstar, almost exclusively limited to running backs. Recently it's been taken one step further. In 1971 George Wells and Joe Theismann trotted out new baby blue boots and Zenon Andrusyshyn brought out his already famous gold kicking shoes. And why not.

True to the mystique, there were people who immediately wanted to know if white shoes were actually better. The best answer I can think of is the analogy to early high school days when hot-rodding your first car was the big thing. Back then I asked a guy why he had put on chrome hubcaps and his answer was, "Because it makes me go faster".

While fans seem to respond readily to a display of showmanship, ballplayers can react negatively even when it's one of their own. Not many players can get

The first tactic employed in a fight . . . . . . grab the other guy's face mask. It's the great neutralizer and usually guarantees not being hurt or hurting in return. It's a standard caution from coaches that in a fight you always keep your helmet on. The other guy is more likely to break his hand than your helmet. There are players who like to fight, but then you can find stupidity anywhere.

119

away with showboating without incurring the wrath of opponents as well as forfeiting the sympathy of teammates.

I think Joe Theismann comes closest to repudiating that claim, but you can't prove it by Greg Barton. Joe and Greg bear enough resemblance that they will put-on the occasional inquisitor by impersonating one another. Following a loss to Hamilton in his rookie year, Joe made a statement regarding the Ti-Cat defence that Hamilton players took as a slight. The next week they took great pains in the return game to impress upon Joe his misinterpretation of their ability. Joe and Greg were alternating at quarterback with each change of possession that day, and when the game was over Greg looked like a bombing victim. In the locker room after the game, Greg just collapsed quietly in his corner, and about all he said was, "I hope nobody else gets mad at Joe. I could get killed".

But the most surprising reaction by players that I've ever seen has been to Ivan McMillan, the Argonaut place-kicker. Ivan has a habit, which I believe is strictly reflex, of jumping in the air and raising his arms if his kick attempt is good. It's a touch of showmanship that adds a little colour to an otherwise routine aspect of the game. In any case I hadn't paid particular attention to it until I started noticing the somewhat negative reaction on the part of the opposing team when Ivan came on for a placement attempt. Such language you wouldn't believe.

The worst thing about it from my standpoint as a blocker up front is the added intensity with which other people try to block our kicks. Our blocking technique on placements requires all the linemen to turn their bodies to the inside, forming a wall from end to end. Being the last man on the line, there's nobody outside of me to protect my ribs, and there has been more than one defensive player to see an easy shot and unload on me.

As in most professional leagues, there are really two seasons in the C.F.L. The first is the regularly scheduled league season, but that's only a prep for the second season, the play-offs leading to the Grey Cup game.

Only three teams are disqualified from Grey Cup competition at the end of the regular season. Two-thirds of the league is still in the running. And, with the possible exception of a battle for unsettled play-off spots as the end of the schedule approaches, there is no time in league play when pressure builds the way it does during play-offs. It really is a different season.

Finishing first in the Conference creates some unusual problems. First-place finishers draw an automatic bye into the finals, the obvious break being no fear of elimination in the first round, which the second and third place finishers must face. But that bye means a two week lay-off at a time when playing conditions are honed pretty fine and a break in routine can throw you off.

After becoming conference winners in 1971 Toronto, however, needed the bye simply to let people heal. We were short bodies due to injuries for much of the last month of the season. We were missing five men from our offensive team at one point and finally had to call Danny Nykoluk out of retirement in order to field an offensive line before the play-offs. For us the rest period was important.

The concept of a two-game total point series as we have in the East is unique in pro sports. It raises a number of questions in regard to strategy.

The option of determining the order for the game goes to the first-place finisher. It can be either first game away, second game home (referring to the stadium at which the game will be held) or the reverse. The advantage of playing the closing portion of the series goes to the home team, so it is standard to play the first game on your opponent's field and return home for the second. In other words, you try to save the home field advantage.

The theory usually expressed by coaches going into the first game is that they are two separate games, and you play to win each one (they are in fact two sixty minute halves). But just break-even on the first game gives you the advantage if you are going home to play the second contest.

Preparing for the second half game against Hamilton in 1971 was the most pressure-filled week of football I've experienced. The big problem was overcoming the Argonaut jinx, the long established habit of blowing the important game. It had actually been established before members of this club got here, but we revived it somewhat with a dismal display of football in the 1970 season, the highlight of which was a season-opening statement by Leo Cahill that, "If we don't win the Grey Cup this year, you should fire the whole coaching staff".

We changed very little from the regular season, adding a couple of new pass plays and counter runs for Hamilton. We felt we could run the ball effectively and exercise ball control, and that's pretty well how it worked out. Hamilton's defensive backfield is the Ti-Cats' strong point and we had less success throwing on them than on any other team in the league. Garney Henley, John Williams, and Al Brenner hurt us bad on pass defence, even

121

Introducing the starting line-up for the Calgary Stampeders:

At centre, number 45
Basil Bark

At left guard, number 57
John Atamian

At right guard, number 51
Granville Liggins

At left tackle, number 62
Dennis Kemp

At right tackle, number 63
Lanny Boleski

At split end, number 74
John Senst

At tight end, number 76
Herm Harrison

At left halfback, number 19
Jesse Mims

At right halfback, number 31
Hugh McKinnis

At slotback, number 17
Rudy Linterman

At flanker, number 72
Gerry Shaw

At quarterback, number 10
Jerry Keeling

though John Williams is primarily noted as one of the best backs in the league against the run.

Going into the second game with a fifteen point lead didn't really ease the pressure. We were fighting ourselves as much as Hamilton.

The game actually varied little from that 15 point differential, and if it was an artistic failure nobody really minded inasmuch as it was an emotional success.

When the gun sounded to end the game I hustled into the dressing room just ahead of an amazing sea of people that swarmed all over the field and everything on it. Nobody else beat the crowd so it was empty beneath the stands. I was hurting from a separated shoulder, but the pressure had built up to such an incredible point that I took the helmet in my hand and just let fly. I watched it bounce off lockers and walls in slow motion, and then there was nothing left. I was too tired to even pick it up.

An awkward position for Hamilton's Garney Henley. He carries the unofficial title of the league's most versatile athlete.

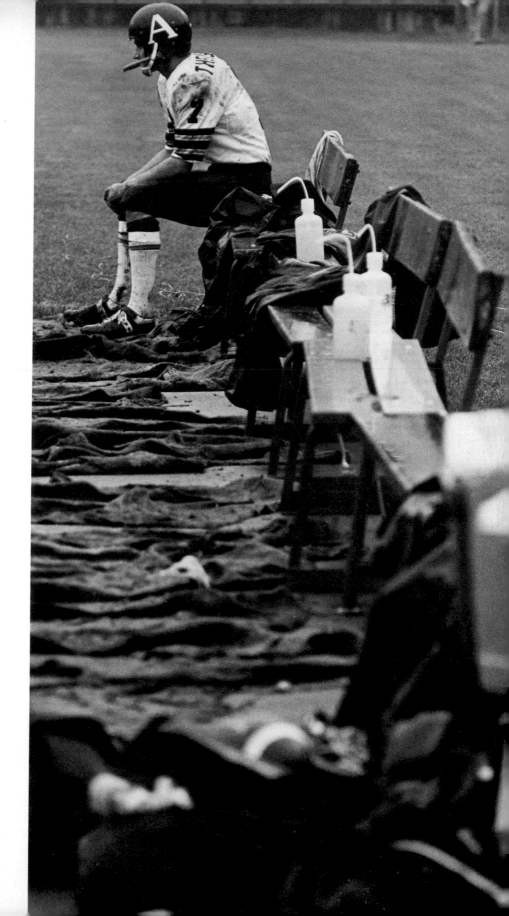

The quarterback is the target. It's as simple as that. A team's ability is measurably reduced if they lose their quarterback. It's the dues paid for receiving the largest contract and the greatest amount of fame. And Joe Theismann pays his dues.

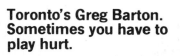

Toronto's Greg Barton.
Sometimes you have to
play hurt.

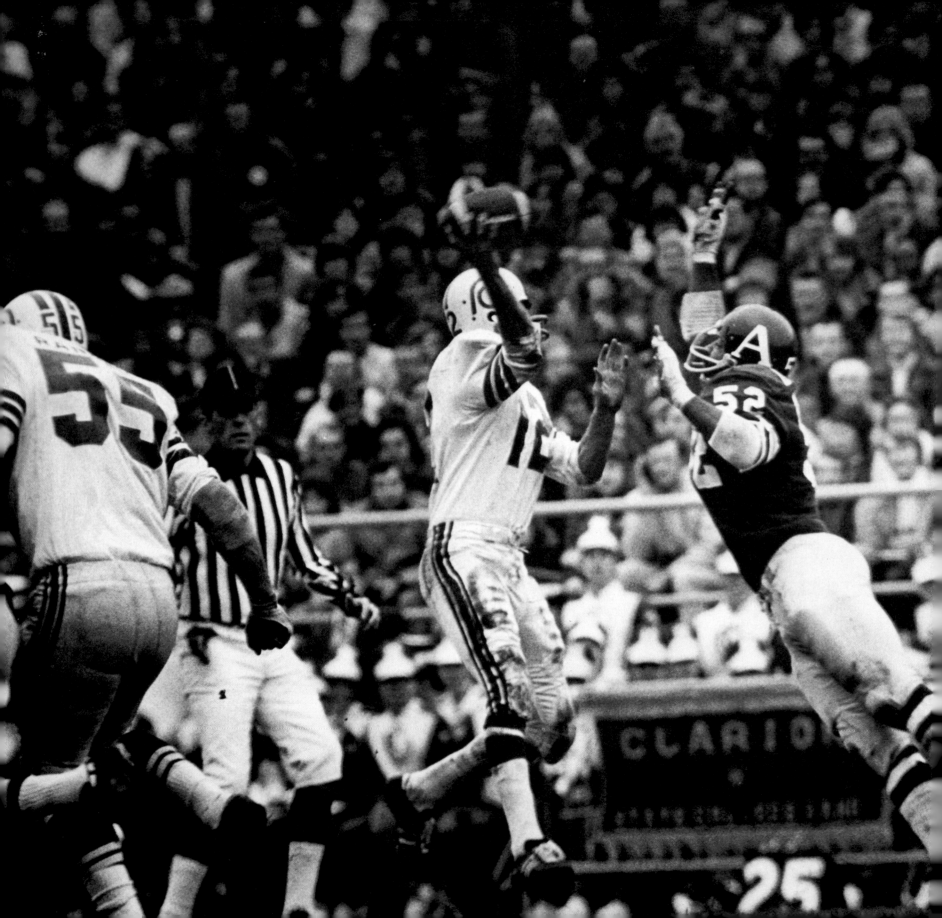

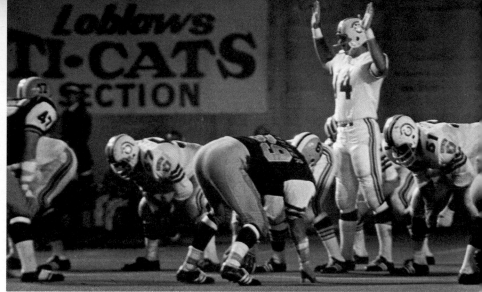

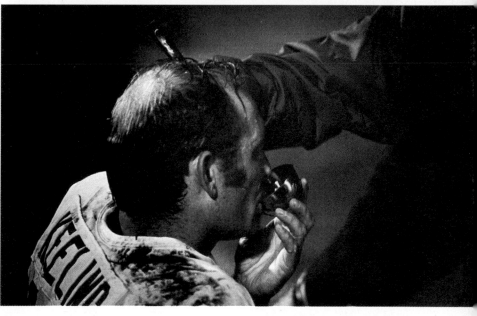

Three moods of a quarterback.
Jim Chasey is about to be punished by Larry Brame, but if he thinks about it he has no chance to complete his pass.

Sonny Wade asks nearly thirty thousand Hamilton fans for quiet so he can go about his job. They're not interested in his request.

Jerry Keeling rests on the sidelines, but not by choice. He just suffered a separated shoulder on the previous series of downs.

The greatest runner in Canadian football, George Reed holds more records than any man in C.F.L. history. He is the all-time leader in career rushing attempts, rushing yardage, touchdowns, and one of only two men to gain more than 10,000 yards.

A defensive back has one responsibility against a pass. See that it isn't completed. In a way the odds are in his favor, because there are three things that can happen to a pass—a completion, an incompletion, or an interception—and two of the three go his way.

Dick Thornton carries it to the ultimate, an interception returned for a touchdown. This return briefly tied him with the all-time professional football record for scoring with interceptions.

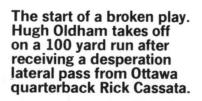

The start of a broken play. Hugh Oldham takes off on a 100 yard run after receiving a desperation lateral pass from Ottawa quarterback Rick Cassata.

136

The hands of a defensive back. Dave Raimey never puts on a uniform, even for picture day, without taping his hands the same way each and every time. For Dick Thornton, one hand is better than two for the receiver.

Overleaf:
Toronto's Leon McQuay . . . all by himself.

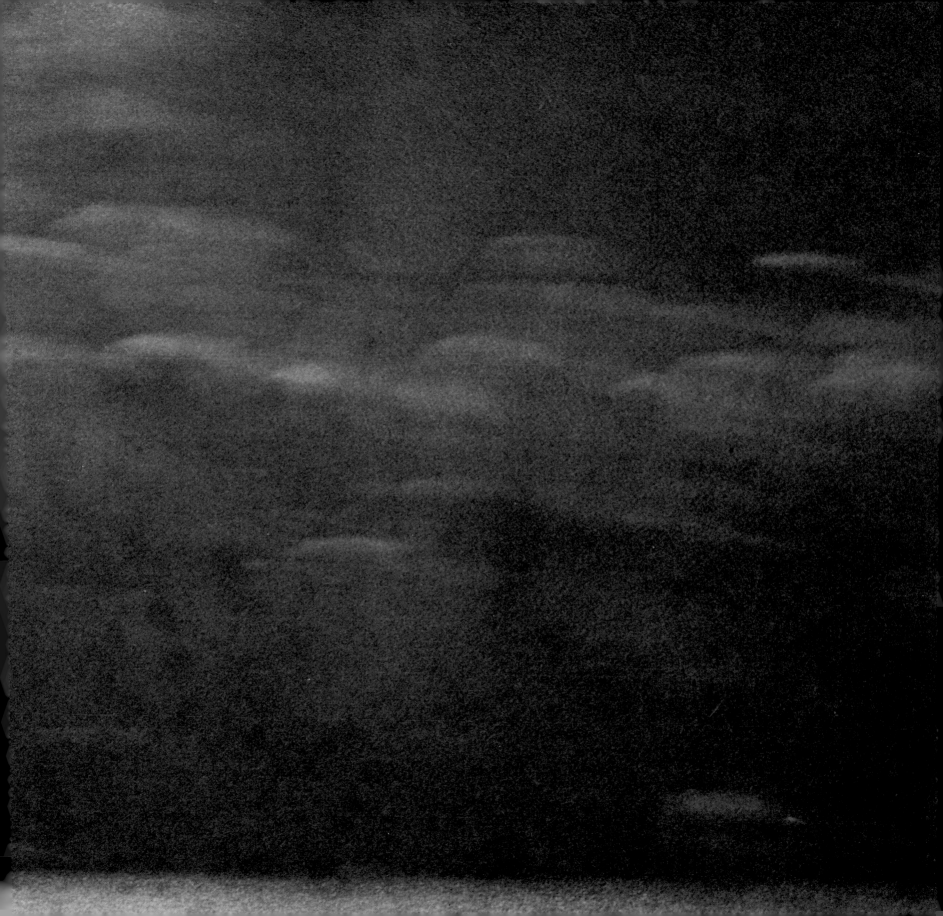

It isn't the means, it's the end. It doesn't make any difference how you bring the ball carrier down, just bring him down. If you want it picture perfect, call Kodak.

142

There are actually two half-time performances going on in the stadium. This one is for the fans, but there's another one going on in the locker room for the players.
Depending on the coach, it may be a relatively calm, organized interruption—nothing more than a cigarette break. But sometimes it's a brief period of chaos, which makes me wish I were up watching the girls' band.

Interviews: The post-game ritual, as important as the game itself. Because for every fan who sees the game in person, twenty-five more will "see" the game through one of these men.
The media people are as different as the players themselves. And they have reputations, just like players. Some you welcome, others you don't. Some you open up to, with others you hedge. Some are accurate, others less so.

Depending on your status, you may or may not have much reason to deal with reporters or sportscasters. If you're a quarterback or running back it's an accepted post-game obligation. If you're a lineman, you might catch a glimpse of them on your way to the shower.

At the far left, Pat Marsden interviews Mike Eben. Left, the king of sartorial splendor, Dick Beddoes. Top, Bob Pennington with Leo Cahill; and above, Sam Etcheverry, surrounded.

147

(Large photo) Toronto's interior line sets up a passing pocket against Edmonton. John Trainor, Charlie Bray and Paul Desjardins drop back to take on Ron Forwick, Greg Pipes and John Lagrone.

(Small photo) A first round draft choice in the N.F.L., Tim Anderson chose Toronto instead to become the highest draft pick ever to sign in Canada.

Linemen are referred to as a lot of things, like "the meat" or "the horses" up front. Essentially, they are the protectors, whether it's the Edmonton linemen protecting the quarterback, Montreal's guards pulling to lead a back on the sweep, or All-Canadian tackle, Bill Frank, the protector, with the league's most valuable player, Don Jonas, the protected.

(Large photo) Of the twelve man, 1971 All Canadian offensive team, five are in the Winnipeg huddle. In front is the league's Most Valuable Player, Don Jonas. The other four are tackle Bill Frank, centre Bob Swift, split end Jim Thorpe, and flanker Bob LaRose.

(Top) Saskatchewan's Ron Lancaster throws from the pocket.

(Bottom) Roughriders' defensive line flanking tackle Ed McQuarters.

The kicking specialist, probably the most unique position in football. Zenon Andrusyshyn's job is simply to kick the ball as far as he can. It's not that easy for the rest of the men who have to learn and rely on the fundamentals of football to understand the need for a specialist, but the need is self-evident. No one else on the team can do the job as well.

The most thankless task on the field is that of returning punts. It's a brutal job. And the story is best told by a punt return man, Jim Copeland, one of the league's best before his retirement in Toronto: "I was 6' 4" when I came into this league. When I retired, I was 5' 8"."

Ottawa's Billy Cooper on one of the few punt returns of any length.

Next page:
(Large photo) "The golden toe" was a title originally reserved for a talented kicker. Toronto's Zenon Andrusyshyn took it a step further.

(Small photo) Ivan McMillan. His kick must have been good.

Away from the game, the actions are as basic as any walk of life. Jim Corrigal is concerned with replacing the 5 to 10 pounds he lost in the game any way he can. Looks don't count.

Argonaut equipment manager, Tommy Bowen, handles repairs with everything from a hammer to needle and thread.

The striking thing about the "get well" message to Leo Cahill's son is the number of players who identify themselves with a football number.

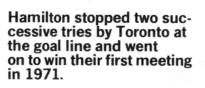

Hamilton stopped two successive tries by Toronto at the goal line and went on to win their first meeting in 1971.

Hamilton's Tommy Joe Coffey, the leading pass receiver in the history of the C.F.L.

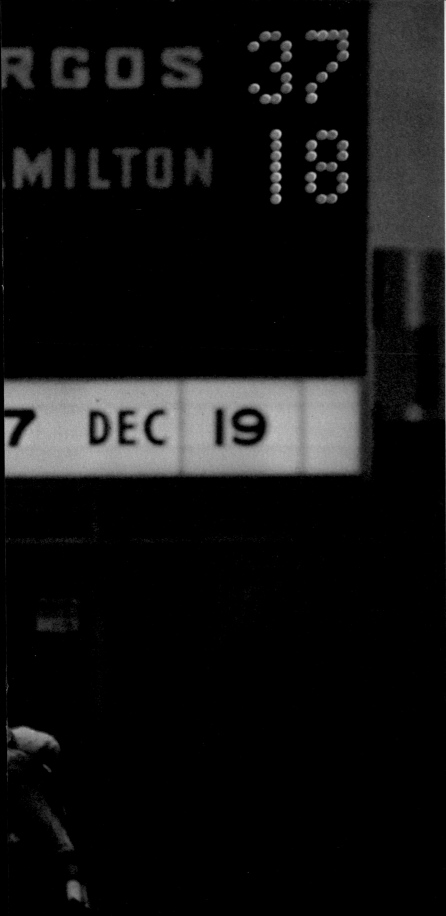

(Large photo) Midway in the second game of the Eastern Conference Finals, Toronto has just about cinched a Grey Cup spot. There will be only one more touchdown scored in this game.

Hamilton went with every strength they could find on this day, even using Garney Henley to return punts. But their frustration is summed up by Wally Gabler after an incomplete third down pass late in the game.

165

Dick Thornton and Marv
Luster near the end of a
play-off victory in Hamilton
for the Grey Cup spot.
Either they're very happy
or they're very cold.

19 Years...Long Enough!

Chapter 7

By 1971 the two teams to have gone the longest without winning a Grey Cup were Calgary and Toronto. Somebody didn't want us to forget how long it had been for the Argonauts. The sign that greeted us in the locker room after we arrived in Vancouver read, "19 years...long enough!"

For me, playing the Grey Cup in British Columbia was ideal. Vancouver is like a second home, so if we couldn't play the game in Toronto this was a beautiful alternative.

The Lions brought me to B.C. in December of 1965, the first time I'd ever been in Canada. And I went crazy. I thought it was one of the most beautiful, friendly places I'd ever been. I brought with me the usual American preconceptions of this country; you know, bring snow shoes and thermal underwear, and don't forget to get pictures of Sergeant Preston.

The stated aim of the visit was to give me an opportunity to see the city, meet some players, and learn a little about the Canadian game. Actually, I knew something of the C.F.L. already because J.I. Albrecht had come to Los Angeles during my third year at U.C.L.A. to talk to me about playing for the Montreal Alouettes. But all things considered in my own mind there was only one real reason for this visit. It was a free vacation.

I signed a C.F.L. contract just 72 hours after arriving.

When we landed in Vancouver on Tuesday for Grey Cup week, the same high feeling was there. So were friends I'd met six years earlier.

From that minute on I never once thought we would lose on Sunday. My mind just accepted as fact the concept that we would win the Grey Cup. Good or bad, it happened. I never felt the psychological disadvantage that goes to the visiting team, which we were for this game, because

169

I never felt like a "visitor".

Even the airport reception worked for me. I got there wearing my standard travelling clothes; jeans, black coat, white tie, and a "lucky" black hat. We were greeted by a number of newspaper photographers, and when the first pictures appeared that afternoon there I was striding along with the descriptions underneath using phrases like "fashion plate" and "sartorial splendor". Since one of our management personnel had already publicly let it be known earlier in the year that he didn't care for the way I dressed, I fervently hoped he would suffer no more than a mild attack of gas.

Everything seemed to fall into place. I felt relaxed, confident, and even more, I was convinced that this was going to be my last game. I'd decided when the regular season ended that if we won the Cup I would retire. There were three main reasons. First, the pressure of living for a couple of years with the rumour that I was about to be canned because of personality conflicts, or my beliefs, or some other crap, was getting to me. I didn't want to go through any more days where I jumped every time the phone rang because I thought it would be someone telling me I'd have to move on again. The second reason was that I'd promised myself I'd get out while I was at my best, not when I'd started downhill and short-changed myself or anyone else. The third reason tied it all together—the Grey Cup. Individual awards are nice, but the ultimate goal is winning the Grey Cup. The odds on winning the Cup are only one in nine each season though, and that's not good. So this looked like the time.

We went directly from the airport to B.C.'s Empire Stadium for our first practice. I was curious to see how everyone else was reacting to the situation, and I was admittedly surprised at the positive feeling that was common to the whole club. As a matter of fact, throughout the week, despite a constant rain, we had the most relaxed, efficient, well-executed workouts of the year.

We'd put in our game plan on Monday's workout in Toronto, and it didn't contain any real changes from the pattern of offence we ran all season. Most western clubs, including Calgary, like to work from a 4-3 defence much of the time and we felt that allowed us to go with our strength, which was to run wide and get Bill Symons and Leon McQuay into the open field. We also put in a couple of counters up the middle to try and neutralize Wayne Harris so he wouldn't be chasing the wide stuff in such a hurry.

We anticipated a majority of zone defences to pass against, another western habit, so we limited our passing game accordingly. We put in a special pass pattern, swinging a back out of the backfield on a deep sideline route, and also a crossing pattern between the slotback and tight end which we'd only used on one previous occasion.

As it turned out, the two special pass plays were both effective to some degree. Each was only used one time and the crossing pattern was good for a gain of over 50 yards, the longest offensive play of the game. On the backfield pattern, Bill Symons broke into the open down the left sidelines, but the ball was overthrown near the goal line. We didn't gain any yardage, but the fans loved it.

The next five days were scheduled around practices, meetings and meals. Normally our routine was breakfast about 9:00, meetings between breakfast and noon, lunch about 12:30, practice in the afternoon, return for dinner, then possibly another meeting or time off until the self-governed midnight curfew.

The curfew came as another surprise. We were conditioned to that 11:00 p.m. curfew, complete with Mickey Mouse bed check, on all our road trips. You have no idea how neurotic a man can become when he has to rush from the library in order to be in bed by 11:00 p.m. or face a stiff fine.

The Argonauts were staying in downtown Vancouver while Calgary had been put up on the outskirts of the city. It seemed to fit with the concept the media gave our encounter. The slick city boys from the East, bad guys wearing black hats, needed the noise and bright lights. The country boys from out West, good guys in white hats, were being shielded from evil. The trouble with that theory is that by the time those country guys get through, it usually takes the big city a week to recover.

The fans themselves were like a human barometer building up for Sunday. We could gauge the distance to game time by the number and condition of the people in town. The day after we arrived our own hotel was packed—with Calgary supporters. We were serenaded by Calgary cheers and fight songs nearly every time we passed through the lobby. But the fact we were there was incidental. People were there to have a good time regardless of any cause. And considering the condition I saw some of them arrive in, I wouldn't have given them a 50—50 chance of surviving until Sunday.

It finally dawned on me before the week was over that the publicity men's whole approach to the Grey Cup is backward. The people don't come to watch the players, the players come to watch the people.

The weather was pretty gloomy all week which, I guess, inhibited the street action a bit, because for all that was going on inside, outside wasn't unusually active.

I'd made the mistake of discounting the madness inherent in Grey Cup week once before. The game was in Ottawa, in 1967. I'd gone there as a reporter for a Toronto newspaper. About midweek I wrote an article expressing disappointment in the festivities and gave it to the Sports Editor to file for me. Naturally that same night people came out of their shells and all hell broke loose. They were swinging on chandeliers, riding horses through lobbies, and generally coming unglued. Fortunately the Sports Editor had taken it on himself to rewrite my copy so the story appeared the next day in a much more accurate form.

With 24 hours to go, the metamorphosis among the players began. There was less joking, even less talk, and tension began to replace the relaxed atmosphere that had been so apparent. The Saturday workout was quick, not so much in duration as in movement. For the first time we were obviously conscious of waiting, the difference between getting ready and being ready. It's a fine point to reach. Get there too soon and by game time you come up flat.

I had purposely avoided talking to my teammates about the attitude of the club. It's a form of superstition, I guess; when things are going well you don't monkey with them. Just let it ride. But every now and then attitudes came out in the damndest ways. For instance, I'd be into something pretty well removed from the Grey Cup and I'd catch myself grinning like a madman. Once at the hotel Dave Raimey just gripped me by the arm and kind of exploded at me, "We are going to win big"! Nothing before, nothing after. But I knew what he felt and I just grinned. It was a great week for grinning. That week was one of only two occasions all year I felt we were really together. It was, to some degree, a throwback to days when it was OK to enjoy yourself rather than to be ruled by professional cool.

Leo Cahill summed up the feeling at the end of Saturday's practice when he told me he thought we could win by 20 points. He didn't mean we were 20 points better than Calgary, but by using all the indications from that week we would play an exceptional game on Sunday. (From a defensive standpoint he was more than right.) The remainder of Saturday was an exercise in patience.

That night Dick Thornton, Zenon Andrusyshyn and I took my parents out to dinner in Vancouver's Chinatown. It was their first trip to Canada and I wanted them to enjoy their stay, but considering the circumstances I knew it would take three of us to make the conversation you would normally expect of one.

Sunday morning we followed our normal pre-game routine. We ate a steak meal at 10:00 a.m., then waited for the bus to take us to Empire Stadium. This is a period in which many players become withdrawn and introspective. I've heard outsiders say they knew they were intruding the minute they came into this environment. The intensity builds to the degree that by game time you can cut chunks out of the air with a knife.

The pre-game warm-up period was changed to accommodate the opening ceremonies. Normally we get out onto the field about 45 minutes prior to kick-off, return to the dressing room for ten minutes, then go back for introductions and the game. This time we were back in the dressing room about a half-hour prior to the kick-off. By game time we'd cooled off enough to negate the value of the warm-ups.

One phase of the ceremonies was the coin-flip to determine the kick-off and receiving teams. When the team captains met on the field, we found out the actual decision had been made earlier by the General Managers. We were going through the motions basically for the ceremonial value. The only decision made on the field was which end the kicking team would defend, a decision based on taking advantage of any possible wind factors.

The game got nothing in the way of help from the condition of the field. For whatever reason, drainage or otherwise, the artificial turf soaked up water until it was like running on a slippery sponge. At the sidelines we were nearly ankle deep. And it was impossible to keep the ball dry despite the efforts of the game officials.

From a Toronto standpoint, offensively it was an exercise in frustration. Calgary gave us the defences we expected, but they were simply out-playing us. We should have been able to run outside on them, but they were not letting us turn the corner. Every time Bill Symons or Leon McQuay got out there, so did Wayne Harris. As difficult as it would become to accept, the fact was that whether the field was wet or dry we were second best that day.

And as great as the Calgary defence played, in the second half our own was better. I didn't read about the game when it was over so I don't know what the statistics were, but I was told in the locker room later that our defence held Calgary to one first down in the second half. If it's true or even close, it was an incredible feat against an offence that good.

The beauty of the game was directly related to two men, the defensive quarterbacks, Wayne Harris and Marv Luster. Their job was to offset the strategy of the offensive quarterbacks they opposed and obviously they did a remarkable job. Even more obviously they were the two dominant individuals in stopping opposition running plays. It might serve to illustrate just what an outstanding performance it was by pointing out that eight of the twelve man All Canadian defensive team were playing in the game.

Only the offensive or defensive signal caller knows why he makes a given decision, but there are rule-of-thumb guidelines for most situations. Early in the second quarter, a long pass play had taken us to about the Calgary 15 yard line. It's common for defences to go into a man-to-man pass coverage that deep, and we were looking for it. Joe Theismann immediately called two quick sprint-out passes, the same play that had scored for us against Hamilton's man-to-man in the play-offs. Wayne Harris kept Calgary in zone and stopped us cold. We had to settle for a field goal.

Despite being down in the second half, I never felt we were going to lose. When we scored with the fumble off a punt return in the third quarter, I thought it was just a matter of time until we broke the game open. Our defence was in control of the game and kept giving us the ball in good field position. I figured we were bound to capitalize on one of the opportunities, if for no other reason than the law of averages.

My faith was still strong in the fourth quarter, but I think it was more inevitability than faith that I was depending on. The attitude on the field was changing though. I could see the defensive team getting more and more frustrated each time they came off the field after getting the ball back for us. It was frustration leading to anger, and they were starting to get on the offence for not moving the ball. I think it reached the stage where some of them, maybe all of them, knew the only way we could win it was if the defence did it on its own. It looked like both points would prove correct, the inevitability and the defensive action, when Dick Thornton intercepted a pass and set us up near Calgary's goal line.

The situation we faced on second down was obvious to any spectator. We had one play to go for a score or to position the ball for a third down field goal attempt, which would have given us a tie and probably sent the game into overtime with momentum on our side. The biggest consideration was positioning the ball for the field goal because Ivan McMillan kicks soccer style and tends to hook the ball to his left. As it was the ball was in close and on the right hashmarks, the worst possible angle on the field for him to kick from.

In the huddle I didn't hear any instructions to the backs about positioning the ball, but everyone was aware of the alternatives. The play called was the obvious choice, a sweep to the wide side. We lined up in a formation that put the tight end on the right, into the short side of the field. On the snap of the ball I headed down and across field looking for a defensive back to block on the play, and never knew there was a fumble until I heard the crowd reaction and saw a Calgary player indicating that it was their ball.

That was the game. It didn't matter that there were two minutes left. We'd been ineffectual all day, and if we couldn't score from that close we obviously weren't destined to score at all. My reaction was strange, and it's no easier to explain or understand today than it was at that moment. Quite honestly I felt nothing. Maybe there was something so subtle that it just doesn't register in my memory, but I didn't feel then, nor do I feel today, any of the bitterness or anger that others felt. I wish I had because frankly I got nothing out of the game. And that's the biggest disappointment of all.

In the locker room a few minutes later, there were two separate teams, just as there had been on the field: a defence that had done far more than was necessary to win, and an offence that had contributed nothing but the loss. Even accepting the axiom, "A team wins and loses together", there were two distinct groups in those first few minutes after the game.

The bitterness and anger were there, but that was a specific reaction of the defensive players. Some of them were still wound up, just as they had been during the game. Gene Mack held the front of his locker and shook it like a man rattling a cage, seething at having to accept the loss. I think he represented the way all the defensive players felt.

I have no idea what went on in the minds of most of the offensive team. Maybe some of them felt the same void I did. I know from comments that came later on there was everything from frustration to confusion to guilt.

While I was getting dressed, someone asked me about retiring. I didn't know what to say then, and I really don't now, except there's no way I can quit on nothing.

The ceremony of Grey Cup.
Maybe more important than
the game itself, the national
involvement in the event is
unique in North American
sports.
I heard about the celebra-
tion of Grey Cup week even
before I heard much about
the Canadian game.

176

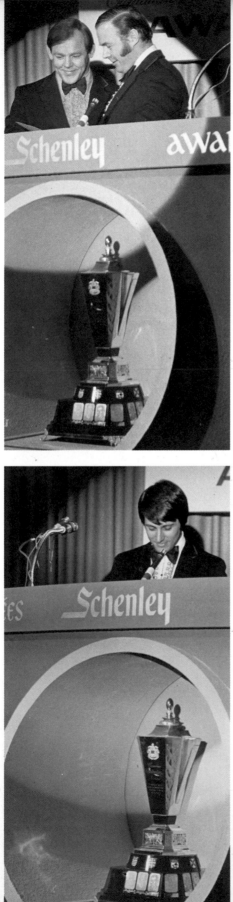

One of the highlights of the 1971 Grey Cup week—the outstanding player awards. Left, Don Jonas, the most valuable player. Above right, Wayne Harris, the outstanding lineman; and below right, Terry Evanshen, the outstanding Canadian. At the far right is C.F.L. Commissioner, Jake Gaudaur.

It's somewhat ironic that in the "character building" sport of football, a manufacturer connected with the leading drug problem in this country is allowed to promote the most honored awards in the league.

Half-time distractions.

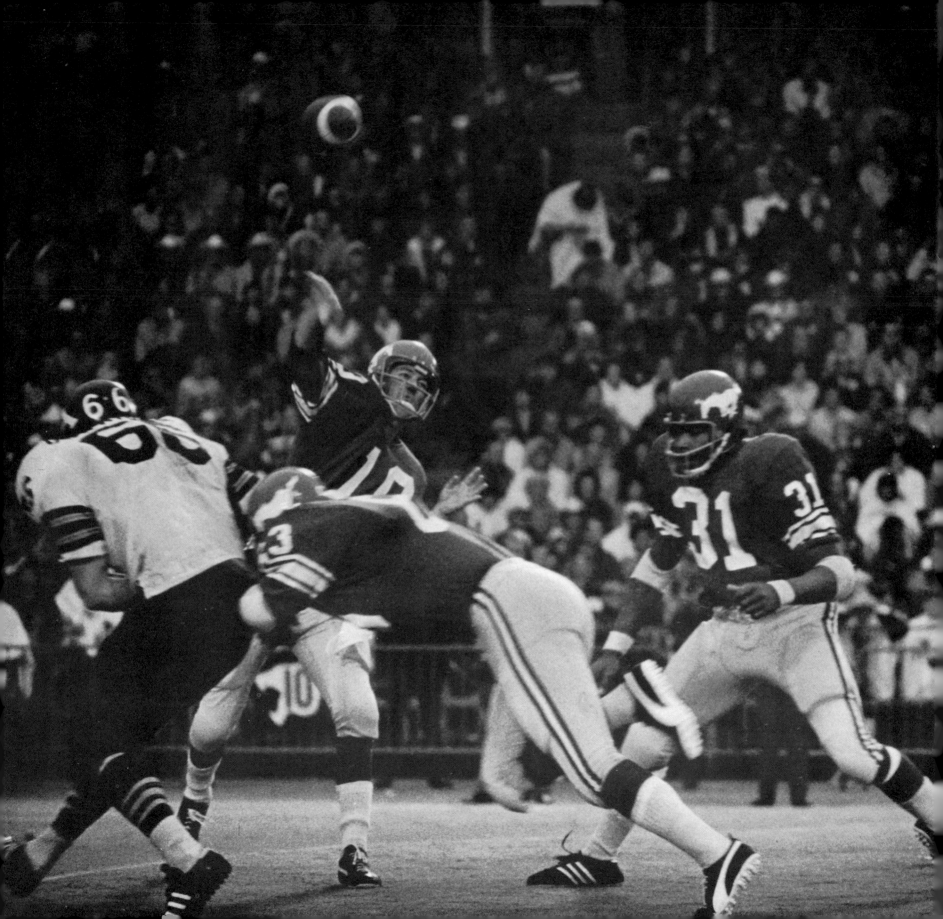

The Grey Cup backfield at work in the first half. They created the only offence of the game in this first thirty minutes. In the second half, they were restricted to just one first down. At the left, quarterback Jerry Keeling; top, halfback Jesse Mims; and above, fullback Hugh McKinnis.

The only two plays of value to Toronto all afternoon. The pass completion at the left was the game's longest offensive play and set up the opening field goal.

At the right, guard Roger Scales scores the Argonauts' only touchdown off the recovery of a fumbled punt. The rest of the afternoon was an exercise in futility.

Symbol of the Grey Cup
champions.

186

The winners' locker room.

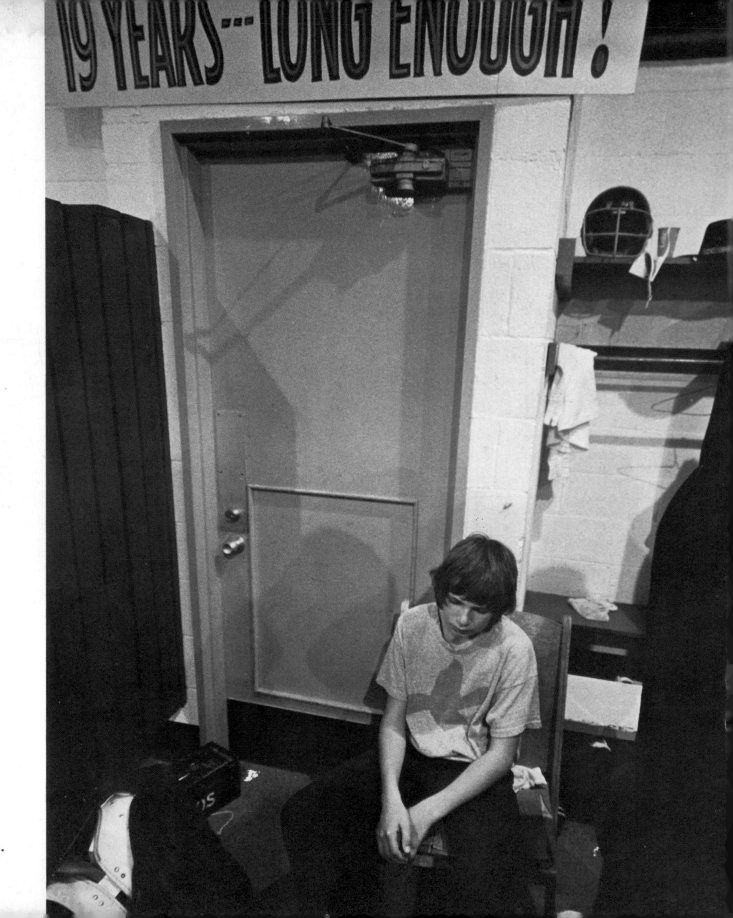

The losers' locker room.

The end.

Acknowledgements

We would like to give added thanks to a number of people for their assistance and encouragement: The Canadian Football League and Commissioner Jake Gaudaur, the Toronto Argonaut Football Club, John Gilchrist, Dave Clark, Lynne Abbey, Don Obe, Fumble, and particularly, Jane Rodmell whose patience, smile, and dining room table were our strength much of the past two years.